The
Thinking
Child

Also available from Continuum

The Thinking Child Resource Book, Nicola Call with Sally Featherstone

The Thinking Child

2nd edition

Brain-based learning for the early years foundation stage

Nicola Call

with Sally Featherstone

continuum

Continuum International Publishing Group

The Tower Building
11 York Road
London
SE1 7NX

80 Maiden Lane,
Suite 704
New York,
NY 10038

www.continuumbooks.com

British Library Cataloguing-in-Publication Data
A catalogue record for this book is available from the British Library.

ISBN: 978-1-855-39472-8 (paperback)

Library of Congress Cataloging-in-Publication Data
Call, Nicola.
 Thinking child : brain-based learning for the foundation stage /
Nicola Call and Sally Featherstone. — 2nd ed.
    p. cm.
 Includes bibliographical references.
 ISBN 978-1-85539-472-8 (pbk.)
1. Cognitive learning. 2. Brain. 3. Effective teaching. 4. Early childhood education. I. Featherstone, Sally. II. Title.

 LB1062.C35 2010

370.15'2—dc22

Typeset by Ben Cracknell Studios
Printed and bound in Great Britain by MPG Books Group Ltd

Some men see things as they are and ask why.
Others dream things that never were and ask why not.

George Bernard Shaw

Contents

Introduction: Understanding the child's brain   **11**

Part One: Preparing the climate and context for learning   **31**

Part Two: Supporting independent learning   **75**

Part Three: Developing brain-based techniques   **107**

Part Four: Teaching for intelligence   **129**

Preface

The Thinking Child is organized according to the principles of brain-based learning. It is divided into an Introduction and then Parts One to Four, which are divided into shorter chapters. Each of these parts is prefaced with a Big Picture, which gives an overview of the contents, and ends with a 'plenary', which suggests some points for reflection.

For the sake of simplification, children are referred to throughout the book as 'he' or 'she', and practitioners as 'she', except where a specific example is being given.

Acknowledgements

Thank you to the many practitioners who so generously shared their ideas and creativity. Writing this book has been a great learning experience for me, and I am extremely grateful to Sally Featherstone for her enthusiasm and commitment to the project. Thanks are also due to Sharon James, Sheila Goode, Heather Anderson, Pat Alsopp, Jenny Barrett, Jill Koops and Siobhan Burrows. The children from Braunstone Frith Infant School in Leicester contributed by providing drawings, photographs and mind maps. The reception class from Seer Green Church of England Combined School in Buckinghamshire contributed many drawings and quotations. The early years staff at Town Farm Primary School in Middlesex provided inspiration and many practical ideas. The teachers, parents and children of Parents Nursery School in Palo Alto, California, provided much inspiration for new material in this second edition.

Above all, thank you to my husband, Josef, for giving the support that enables me to combine writing with being a mother. Thank you to my children Alysia, Rebecca and Alexander for giving me continual first-hand experience of the needs of young children as they allow me to share their joy in discovering more about their world. My children are my greatest teachers: may they live and learn in a world of positive experiences, and may all their dreams be realized.

Understanding the child's brain

The Big Picture

In this section you will:

Step 1: Read the answers to some 'frequently asked questions' about brain-based learning

Step 2: Visit a pre-school, a nursery class and a reception class where the practitioners work using brain-based learning techniques

Step 3: Meet four young children in these three settings, who will become quite familiar to you as you read on through the book

Step 1: Answering some frequently asked questions

What exactly is 'brain-based learning'?
'Brain-based learning' is a term used to describe how to apply theories about the brain to help children to maximize their potential for learning. Once you understand the theory behind brain-based learning, you can put its various aspects into practice and enhance the learning of the children in your care.

Is this a scheme that means that I have to start to work more formally with the children in my setting?
Absolutely not! *The Thinking Child* is not a scheme or a curriculum. This book simply offers a method of working that derives from an understanding of the current research

into how the brain develops. We know that young children learn best through play, and the techniques that are described in this book should be incorporated into the work done in the Early Years Foundation Stage (EYFS).

Will I need additional resources to implement these strategies in my setting?
You should not need to make any major purchases to implement the techniques that are described in this book. Most of your work will simply involve being creative with the resources that are already available.

Will implementing these techniques increase my workload?
Using these techniques will probably involve different work, but not necessarily more work. Understanding the new evidence about how children learn should lead to a more informed way of teaching. In fact, because you will be enhancing the learning of the children in your setting, the same time commitment should lead to far greater productivity.

If I implement these strategies, will it necessitate major changes of policy within my setting?
Implementing the techniques in this book should not necessitate any additional paperwork or radical alteration of current policies. Practitioners find that once they gain a better understanding of the brain and how it works, they may need to reconsider and improve upon some of their ways of working, but this does not necessitate major policy changes in most cases, nor should it necessitate deviation from current curriculum guidance.

How do these learning techniques fit in with the Primary Strategy for Literacy and Numeracy?
Different practitioners implement the Primary Strategy for Literacy and Numeracy according to their individual situations. In Part Two we discuss how to structure the more formal sessions, but brain-based principles, such as using movement, music, and visual, auditory and kinesthetic learning, apply equally to the formal and less formal sessions.

Are these ideas appropriate for all settings and schools?
Having a better understanding of the most up-to-date evidence about how children learn will help a childminder improve on her practice just as much as the headteacher of a large nursery school, or a practitioner in a Children's Centre or extended provision. The methods described in this book are equally applicable to any child in any setting.

How do these techniques fit in with the demands upon practitioners, such as the EYFS Guidance and Every Child Matters?
Because these techniques are all derived from the latest understanding of child development and brain research, they do not need to be adapted or tailored to keep up with the demands of current legislation. Instead, they should underscore all the work that you do, meaning that you can respond more effectively to new challenges as they arise.

Is this just the latest educational fad?
Brain-based learning is not a 'fad'. This is not to say that there have not been some fads emerge as the concept of brain-based learning became better known, but these faddish trends should not negate the importance of understanding the latest evidence of how children learn. In this book, you will find descriptions of the current research into how the brain functions, along with suggestions of techniques that will help to maximize children's learning. It is simply not possible to learn in a way that is not brain-based!

Step 2: **Let's meet a brain**

‘ To have a good brain, first you have to exercise and then you must eat lots of apples. ,

Owen, aged five

In this chapter we are going to meet a human brain and learn a little about how it works. In other words, we're going to get the hard bit over first – but don't let this put you off! The intent is simply to provide a very basic overview of the major components of the human brain. Later, we will use this information as a reference point, allowing us to more easily visualize what is happening inside the minds of children as they undergo the enriching, brain-based learning experiences described in this book.

‘ *When it comes to building the human brain, nature supplies the construction materials and nurture serves as the architect that puts them together.* ,

Ronald Kotulak[1]

Over the years, experts have developed numerous theories about the nature of intelligence and its relationship with two powerful and sometimes conflicting forces: nurture and nature. Recently, researchers have made more progress than ever before, and the mysteries of intelligence have begun to unravel. For instance, scientists have now managed to count the numbers of brain cells within specific areas of the brain and can calculate the phenomenal number of interconnections that are made as these cells communicate with one another. Scientists now have technology that allows them to look deep inside the living, functioning brain and observe electro-chemical activity as thoughts and emotions are developed and processed. As the mysteries of the brain are unravelling, many long-held theories are being disproved and new ones developed.

What is becoming increasingly clear is that the first few years of life are the most critical in terms of physical brain development. The most significant period for the wiring of the brain is during these years. Typically, this process is nearly complete by the age of 12. We now know that there are various windows of opportunity for learning between birth and the age of three or four, but that nature gives a child's brain a second chance between the ages of about four and 12. This means that an enormous responsibility lies in the hands of parents and early years practitioners.

At the micro level, the human brain consists of about one hundred billion nerve cells, called *neurons*. These neurons can be thought of as very simple data processors, which work together to solve a particular problem as it is presented to the brain. The human brain is able to easily perform tasks that the largest, most expensive computers today find impossible to accomplish. Some everyday examples of these tasks include understanding spoken human language, identifying objects by sight, sound, smell, touch and taste, and writing and understanding literature. Whereas computer processors typically attack problems sequentially, one piece at a time, the power of the human brain lies in its ability to orchestrate the activities of billions of individual neurons working together. The human brain can be likened to a symphony conductor.

Neurons develop *axons* for transmitting information to other neurons and *dendrites* for receiving information. As patterns of thought are first initiated and subsequently repeated, the participating neurons continually process and communicate. In doing so, they build stronger and more direct axon-to-dendrite pathways – called *synapses* – to other neurons. In other words, with repeated stimulation, these connections become ever stronger and more established, and the brain has in effect 'learned' how to solve that particular problem. At this point, the brain is ready to undertake further learning. Interestingly, those neurons that do not generate synapses quite literally die off.

At the macro level, the brain can be thought of in three parts: the *brain stem*, the *limbic system* and the *cerebral cortex*. These parts of the brain are divided again into specific areas, each with an individual and complex role to play. Some areas process information gleaned from the senses, while others process different aspects of our emotional responses. Some are responsible for laying down certain types of memory, while others help us to 'read' cues from other people and make appropriate emotional and physical responses.

The brain stem is physically the lower part of the brain, which connects to the spinal cord. The brain stem and cerebellum are often referred to as 'the reptilian brain'. This part of the brain is primarily responsible for the body's survival systems: for regulating our life support mechanisms such as heart rate and breathing, and for what is known as the 'flight or fight' response to perceived danger. Under stress, our basic survival instincts kick in and we produce chemicals that put the body under heightened alert. During these times of stress, higher order thinking becomes derailed, and learning cannot take place effectively. It is for this reason that ideal learning environments are those that reduce a child's stress level to its absolute minimum.

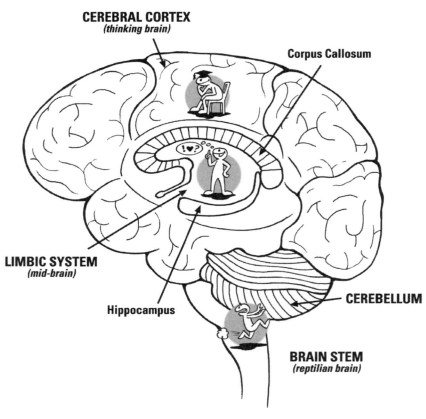

Between the brain stem and the cerebral cortex is the limbic system. This is sometimes referred to as the *mid-brain*. The limbic system consists of several structures that manage our emotions and are responsible for some aspects of memory. The lower structures of the limbic system control our more basic emotional responses, while the higher ones are responsible for making a more intellectual response. For example, if you were to hear an unfair criticism of your work, the lower areas of the limbic system would deal with your more spontaneous responses such as blushing or shaking, while the higher areas would process the social issues that might help you to make a measured response to your critic. This makes sense, as the higher parts of the limbic system are in closer contact with the cerebral cortex, where the most sophisticated thought processes take place.

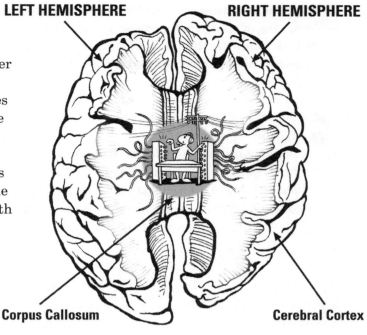

LEFT HEMISPHERE   **RIGHT HEMISPHERE**

Corpus Callosum   **Cerebral Cortex**

The cerebral cortex is the largest part of the brain. It is sometimes referred to as 'the thinking brain'. The cerebral cortex is physically separated into two hemispheres, rather like two halves of a walnut. Scientists are constantly discovering more about the left–right relationship and the very specific roles that each area undertakes. Often new information about the different hemispheres is discovered through studies of people who have suffered brain damage. For example, researcher Tatiana Schnur from Rice University in Texas studied a group of healthy people alongside a group who had suffered strokes.[2] She wanted to know more about the process that occurs when we choose one word above another – for example, selecting the word 'warm' to describe the temperature of water. If we were to say the word 'wet' instead of 'warm', we would not convey the correct meaning, even though the word 'wet' can pertain to water. Many stroke patients encounter difficulties with word selection, and are described as 'Broca's aphasics'. Schnur found that successful decision-making when choosing words depended upon the health of the left inferior frontal gyrus, where Broca's area is located. When that area of the brain is damaged, the patient cannot make efficient choices about word usage. Other aspects of language processing happen in different areas of the brain, and nothing happens in complete isolation. We are complex creatures, and in order for us to function normally, each part of each hemisphere needs to do its own job and the two hemispheres need to communicate effectively through the *corpus callosum,* which is like a super-highway through which messages travel.

In recent years, pop culture has created the concept of 'left-brain learners' and 'right-brain learners', as if individuals can be categorized according to the side of their brain that supposedly dominates their thinking. This is a gross oversimplification. Nobody is a 'leftie' or 'rightie' when it comes to brain use. It would be very foolish of us to try to categorize children before we even know if they are left or right handed, especially as the notion of brain-handedness is nonsense! While everyone has strengths and weaknesses and learning preferences, each area of each person's brain is used for many different and very specific functions. As they interact with each other, they are performing something like an incredibly elaborate and complex dance, which scientists are only just beginning to understand. Nobody's brain performs this 'dance' in only one hemisphere, and so if asked what sort of brain you have, you can answer very confidently that your brain is ambidextrous.

Throughout this book you will find references to various parts of the brain along with explanations of research that supports the theory behind brain-based learning techniques. What is perhaps startling is the fact that altering a child's environment and breadth of experiences can actually make a radical difference to his or her IQ level at a later age:

> *Within a broad range set by one's genes, there is now increasing understanding that the environment can affect where you are within that range. . . . You can't make a 70 IQ person into a 120 IQ person, but you can change their IQ measure in different ways, perhaps as much as 20 points up or down, based on their environment.*

Frederick Goodwin[3]

As we become more informed about the functioning and capability of the brain, we can become increasingly effective in helping children to learn. Scientists are helping to inform our practice more now than ever before. It is an exciting time to be involved with the learning of young children, and the adventure is only just beginning.

Step 3: Meeting the children in their settings

Arriving at the setting

> *We teachers can only help the work going on, as servants wait upon a master.*

Maria Montessori[4]

Today we are going to spend some time in an early years setting where the staff have been using brain-based learning techniques for several years. This setting consists of a pre-school situated in the church hall, and a nursery and reception class in the school next door. The practitioners here enjoy a strong relationship and work to ensure good continuity and progression. We will meet four children: George, who attends the pre-school, Carrie, who

is the oldest child in the nursery, and Kishan and Samantha, who are both in the full-time reception class.

These four children are not 'case studies'. They are fictitious characters who are used throughout the text to illustrate how learning is affected by the choices made by adults around them. Although our focus is on the EYFS, at times we will draw upon research into very early child development, including foetal development. This is because we often need to understand the significance of what has gone before in order to make sense of where the child currently 'is'. What happens in the earliest weeks, months and years will shape the brains of the children who enter our settings.

Our first stop is at the church hall, where the pre-school session is just beginning. A practitioner greets each child by name, including George, who is one of our four children. The children are encouraged to take off their coats and organize their bags independently into labelled boxes at the door. George hurries over to greet his friend Peter, who has just arrived with his mother. George chats to Peter as his mum helps him onto the carpet from his buggy. Peter is now able to take part in most pre-school activities with help, but gets very stiff when he sits in the buggy. His key person comes over to greet him

and to talk to his mother about the plans for the day. The atmosphere is calm and serene, in part due to the quiet strains of Beethoven playing on the CD player at the back of the hall.

Children then look at the weekly planner and today's To Do list on the free-standing whiteboard. The children are being given the Big Picture as they see that this week they are going to investigate sponges. There are sponges everywhere: giant sponges in the water tray, triangular sponges in the painting trays and big yellow sponges in buckets next to a 'Car Wash' sign. The parents settle their children to activities before saying goodbye. Peter's mum and two parents are staying to help for the morning. George's mother also stays for a while. She settles down to read a few stories with a group of children.

Let's meet George

George is the one of the youngest in the pre-school, which he attends three mornings per week. He is glad that his mother is staying for a while this morning, as it has taken him some time to settle into the pre-school routine. To look at George, you would not realize that he is one of the youngest children in the room. At just one ounce less than 10lbs at birth, George has always been large for his age. His father is pleased that George was a larger baby, because he has read recent claims that bigger babies are more intelligent!

In August 2001, the *British Medical Journal* published details of a study that showed that there is a link between birth weight and IQ, even when factors such as the family's socio-economic background are taken into account. The researchers found that those who weighed more scored higher in intelligence tests than those who weighed less.[5]

The pre-school leader also read accounts of this research, but she didn't create a new column in her record book to record each child's birth weight! For her, the most interesting point was that the study showed that there seemed to be a vital point at about the age of eight, where a child's test scores had the greatest significance regarding his future attainment. This brought home to her the enormous responsibility of early years educators.

George is the only child in his family and he receives considerable attention from his extended family. This will most likely mean that George's brain is larger than that of a child who has only experienced an impoverished environment.

In the nineteenth century, Charles Darwin conducted research on the brain sizes of domestic rabbits versus those who lived in the wild:

‘ *I have shewn that the brains of domestic rabbits are considerably reduced in bulk, in comparison with those of the wild rabbit or hare; and this may be attributed to their having been closely confined during many generations, so that they have exerted their intellect, instincts, senses and voluntary movements but little.* ’

Charles Darwin[6]

Since Darwin's time, researchers have confirmed his findings by showing that laboratory animals kept in enriched environments grow a thicker cerebral cortex than animals kept in impoverished surroundings. If a child is brought up in an impoverished environment, her brain suffers. From the earliest age, even before birth, exposure to positive interactions begins to establish the neural circuitry in the brain for future success.

After birth, the billions of neurons begin to communicate with one another to form the complex 'wiring' of the brain. These synapses form at the astounding rate of approximately three billion per second, meaning that by the time George was eight months old, his brain had formed about one thousand trillion connections. When a child is exploring his world and is curious, his brain cells generate numerous connectors, which sprout like tiny tree branches. Brain cells that are not stimulated soon die. It truly is a case of 'use it or lose it'.

Thankfully, George does not suffer from any lack of stimulation, and his brain is still developing at an astounding rate. But George did suffer as a newborn baby from colic. His grandmother spent time each day giving him infant massage. She didn't realize that she was also helping his physical growth and his brain development.

It has been found that children who are rarely touched are physically smaller than their peers. American researchers Schanberg and Field studied the effect that touch has on premature babies. They found that if the babies were held and their backs were rubbed, their levels of stress hormones decreased and their growth rate doubled.[7] Tactile experience also affects brain development. Experiments with monkeys have shown that repeated touching of the fingers produces a larger corresponding area in the cerebral cortex.

Furthermore, tactile experience affects emotional development. In the United States, Dr William Sears has spearheaded a campaign for greater awareness for the importance of touch for children. His style of parenting has become known as 'attachment parenting'. Other experts such as Steve Biddulph comment on this difference between our culture and what he calls 'wiser cultures':

Notice how babies from many of the wiser cultures are carried around in slings and carrybags? One Balinese tradition is the first 'setting down to earth' of a new baby – it does not take place until the child is six months old. Before this it is never out of somebody's arms![8]

A baby that is carried in this way is automatically stimulated by the activity and conversation of the adult, so promoting his language and social development. Moreover, he is assured of enough touching to fully stimulate his developing nervous system. George has obviously benefited from the physical reassurance and attention that he receives at home. He is a quiet, gentle and tactile child. He is somewhat wary of new situations and often wants to follow the lead of other children, but his key person reassures his parents that this is quite common for summer-born children. After all, some of the other children have had almost a year's headstart on George! George clambers onto his key person's lap when his mother leaves. Fortunately the pre-school practitioners welcome physical touch from the children and George is always assured of a warm reception.

We leave the pre-school for now, and cross the playground into the main school building, where we are going to visit the nursery class. As we are about to enter the room, we see two of the nursery children on their way to the office with the register. They are holding hands and are looking up at the pictures of animals along the corridor walls. They almost collide with the returning pair from reception class, who are looking for red triangles on the ceiling.

We go into the nursery, where the children are engaged in an active phonics session, moving rhythmically to songs and rhymes and using all their senses to enhance their learning. As they get ready for assembly, their teacher chooses not to ask these young children to make a formal line. Instead, they have been taught to make their way to the door in a calm manner. This is where we meet Carrie, who is drawing a large letter 'C' in the air.

Let's meet Carrie

Carrie's mother calculated that she was due to be born on August 31st but Carrie did not arrive until September. This means that she is one of the oldest children in her year group. Research into the advantages and disadvantages for the oldest versus the youngest in the class tends to be complex. Summer-born children often seem to make as much progress as their older peers over a year, but it is important to take their 'starting point' into account. This is now being recognized in the UK, with recommendations that children who are born in the summer months should start their reception year in the autumn term, thus having the same time in school as all children in their year group, whenever they were born.

There is no simple solution to this problem, however. The 2007 study *When You Are Born Matters* found that a September start in school makes '*only a modest positive contribution to test scores and only at early Key Stages*' and suggests that a possible solution might be to offer greater flexibility over school start dates, along with a re-think about when children should become eligible for free nursery education.[9] The researchers found that there is a significant 'August birth penalty' that lasts right until the age of 18, with summer-born children even being less likely to enter higher education than their winter-born peers.

Because Carrie was born late, she was not a 'summer-born' child after all. Her birth was straightforward and she had an Apgar score of nine when tested one minute after her arrival. Although parents are always relieved when their baby receives a healthy Apgar score, it is in no way a baby IQ test. Yet it is astounding to reflect on the fact that at birth a baby has about one hundred billion brain cells or neurons. Until recently it was believed that after birth the human brain was incapable of manufacturing more neurons. We now know that this is wrong. Scientists at the Salk Institute in California have proved that mature people do create additional neurons in a section of the *hippocampus*.[10] This finding has excited researchers with its potential for treating disorders involving neuron damage.

Fascinating Fact

Dr Virginia Apgar devised the Apgar score in 1952. Newborn babies are assessed immediately after birth for skin colour, muscle tone, heart rate, reflexes and respiration, and given a score of 0, 1 or 2 for each.

Carrie's hundred billion brain cells had been produced at the staggering rate of over four thousand per second, if averaged out for her nine months in the womb. But this was the last thing on her mother's mind as, within moments of birth, she held her to her breast. Carrie's mother was convinced of the health benefits of breastfeeding, but had not realized that scientists have now proved that breastfeeding increases a child's IQ, or perhaps more accurately, that bottle-feeding can potentially lower a child's IQ. In a study in 1999, researchers at the University of Kentucky found that even after breaking out socio-economic factors, breastfed babies scored higher in IQ tests than formula-fed infants.[11]

Fats are an important component of the brain cell membrane and the myelin sheath around each nerve, and breast milk provides the exact types and proportions of fats such as the fatty acid DHA to maximize an infant's brain development. In her first year, Carrie's brain tripled in size, and during this stage of rapid central nervous system growth, her brain used 60 per cent of the total energy that she consumed.

Carrie's mother still takes care to monitor her daughter's diet and to limit the amount of artificial food additives that Carrie consumes. Carrie attends a breakfast club because her mother, who is a single parent, has to commute several miles to work. The children at breakfast club are fed a healthy balanced meal. The teachers also provide healthy snacks and drinks during the day, realizing that young children perform better when allowed to eat little and often and when they are fully hydrated. As Carrie joins hands with her friend ready to make her way to assembly, we move on to visit the reception class next door.

The reception class entered school earlier to the lively sound of Bill Haley's *Greatest Hits*. The teacher welcomed each child by using his name and giving him eye contact. If she was drawn into conversation by a parent, she used the child's name soon afterwards. This is a school policy. The teacher also recalls small details of children's lives – details that might seem insignificant to an adult, but can be major for the child. As we walk into the room, she is asking Carmen about her dental appointment last Friday.

Once the children have said goodbye to their parents, the teacher changes the music to a CD of relaxing ocean sounds. For the few minutes before assembly, the children practise writing their names in the air with their hands. Some write the initial letters, while others write their full name. A few use home-made 'magic wands'. The children write in the air with their eyes closed, using right hand, then left hand, then using both hands. Soon it is time to line up.

The children listen carefully to the teacher. 'Those of you with long brown hair can line up first,' she says, slowly and deliberately. 'That's almost right, Jake, you do have brown hair. But is it long – or is it short?' Jake sits back down. 'Now those with short brown hair may line up,' she continues, and Jake joins the line.

Reception class arrive at assembly, having counted ten red triangles and eight blue squares on the corridor ceiling on their way. The children who are seated in the hall are

not bored; there is plenty to look at while they wait. The practitioners encourage the children to 'dance' to music with their hands in the air, or to look at a Monet print at the front of the hall. There is no static display in this school; there are always new things to stimulate children's thinking. Before assembly ends, there is the sound of applause as the achievements of individuals and groups are recognized. Music is then heard again through the corridors, and the children leave quietly.

Back in the classroom, the reception children begin one of their literacy sessions. A group of children listen to the teacher giving the Big Picture. When she has finished her explanation, she asks if every child is 'on a green light'. A few are still 'on amber' so she repeats the explanation until everyone is confident that they understand. In this session, the children at one table are working on green sheets of paper. 'Green is for go go go!' a little girl says to the child sitting next to her.

Groups of children are working in different areas of the classroom. It is difficult to tell which children are involved in adult-led activities and which are engaged in child-initiated learning, and an observer may describe what many of them are doing as 'play'. That is because their teacher recognizes that play, for young children, is indeed work. One group, wearing hairnets, are cooking plastic vegetables and writing recipes in the home corner. Five or six others are touring the room with clipboards, deeply involved in an imaginary game that involves collecting red items, drawing them, and taking notes. One of these children goes into the home corner, where he holds a deep conversation with the hair-netted cooks about how to spell 'red pepper'.

The Three As are **Acknowledgement, Approval** and **Affirmation**, and are discussed in depth on pages 61–64.

The groups of children concentrate well for five or six minutes, when it is time for the teacher to help some of them to refocus. Whenever there is a drop in concentration or a child starts to go off-task, *The Three As* system of *Acknowledgement, Approval* and *Affirmation* is used. Some of the children are now ready for their first brain break.

The classroom assistant leads the children in the 'cross crawl' exercise. Children will take regular brain breaks throughout the session, often coinciding with beginning a new type of activity. Some of these breaks will be structured Brain Gym®[12] activities; while others might be action songs and rhymes or simple movements. One of the practitioners remains close to Madeline, who may need help in controlling her movements during these periods.

Towards the end of this session we meet Kishan, who is pouring himself a glass of water. He then settles back down to his task. After another ten minutes, he goes to the mat to demonstrate 'good listening' before his teacher sends the class out to play.

Let's meet Kishan

If you ask Kishan how old he is, he will tell you, 'I'm almost five-and-three-quarters'. He has been in reception class for two terms. Kishan didn't attend either the pre-school or the nursery class, because he was settled at the full-time day care centre that he attended from the age of three months.

Kishan's family is bilingual. His parents are the first generation of their families to be born in the United Kingdom, and speak Bengali and English fluently. Like countless others, Kishan will become fluent and fully literate in both languages with little difficulty. Years ago, it was considered a disadvantage for a child to speak a second language at home. More recently, bilingualism has become fashionable, in part due to the popular belief that it makes children more intelligent. This has led to a myriad of second-language products, with some making fairly extreme claims about their potential for raising children's IQ. There is evidence that bilingualism can raise abilities in some specific areas of functioning, such as meta-linguistic awareness, but there is little evidence to support claims that it can make a baby 'smarter'. In any case, becoming fluent in a second language requires continual one-to-one communication with a native speaker. Toys, DVDs, computer programs and CDs may be an enjoyable way of learning vocabulary, but they will not increase a child's IQ. There is no need to invest in such toys as a 'Bilingual Talking Videophone' or a 'Bilingual Alphabet Drum'!

There are what scientists call 'sensitive periods' for learning, and most of these periods, including that for learning language, occur during the first five years of life. It is essential that babies hear the phonemes of any language that their parents wish them to speak while they are very young. Children's ability to learn multiple languages at a very early age is incredible. But if they have not heard the phonemes of a language by six months, their ability to identify the unfamiliar sounds diminishes fast; for example, between the letters 'l' and 'r'. Children need to be exposed very early to the maximum amount of language if their ability to learn is to be fully exploited.

Any impairment to hearing may significantly impact a child's language development. Children with hearing loss are often more impulsive than their peers, and can tend to be more physical and even aggressive. Kishan's behaviour can sometimes be described as rambunctious and even challenging. Because he is a boy, he is at least three times as likely as the girls in his class to be diagnosed as having behaviour difficulties such as ADHD. His teacher is working to help him to manage his impulsivity. In her opinion, Kishan's behaviour is normal for a child with a highly inquisitive nature and boundless energy!

ADHD = Attention Deficit and Hyperactivity Disorder. We discuss ADHD on page 85.

Fortunately, Kishan's teacher sees his energetic nature as a positive trait. She uses *The Three As* motivational system to help her to manage Kishan's boisterous behaviour. Kishan's brain may have a proportionately larger right hemisphere than Carrie or Samantha's. This possibly contributes to his strengths in activities that involve

manipulating objects through three dimensions and spatial awareness. Out in the play area, he has taken charge of a mixed group of children as they build a dinosaur from some big cardboard boxes. Other children ride bikes, while others play in the sand and water trays. Another group of children are in dressing-up clothes and are using a wooden platform as a stage for their game of *The Three Bears*. The play area is full of activity, with a supply of equipment for physical and imaginative play. There is plenty for everyone, and the teacher suggests, directs and organizes games for those who do not do so independently. She participates and communicates with the children, recognizing and encouraging good social skills.

The reception children go back into the classroom and sit down for their snack. The teacher points to a poster on the wall as she reminds them of the rules for 'good sitting' as the fruit is handed out. They then move on to maths. They start by doing 'body maths'. Alongside verbal instructions, the teacher uses visual cues. Today she shows cards with bold pictures of different shapes. The children are asked to represent each shape with their bodies, first individually and then in groups. Madeline giggles as her key person works with her to gently represent some of the shapes using her own body and Madeline's hands and arms. As we leave the reception classroom to go back to see what is happening in the nursery, we can hear the teacher saying, 'That's a very accurate square, Kishan. Now can you turn it into a triangle?'

Meanwhile, over in the nursery, the children are making a giant mind map about 'water' on the carpet. The word 'water' is printed in bold letters on a card in the centre of the map, and the children are working to organize pictures and related objects around it. These are joined with strips of card that indicate the relationship between concepts, such as a toy watering can being linked with a strip of card to a picture of a plant. Sponges feature in two places on this hands-on map; near the words 'bath' and 'washing up'. The teacher throws a new word into the discussion: 'absorb'. A round of applause celebrates the group's success as the mind map is complete for today.

The nursery children then move away to take part in different activities. Before they go, they tell the teacher what they plan to do next. She simply nods or gives a 'thumbs-up' to some children, but with others she asks a question or makes a suggestion about their plan. Some children put on coats and go outside. Others choose to stay indoors. Activities out of doors mirror the work going on inside. A box of hats and a reel of bus tickets have been left in a basket near the bricks. Soon a group of children start work on building a bus, while a second group organizes the sponges ready to give the bus a wash! Carrie and her friend fetch marker pens and sheets of card to make a sign for the bus stop. Very soon an elaborate game has begun. The nursery nurse watches and facilitates, while allowing the creativity and spontaneity of the children to lead the game.

When we leave the nursery and walk back to watch the pre-school group, we find that George and his friends are busy too. The pre-school shares use of the church hall with several other local groups and everything has to be put out and packed away each day, but this does not reduce the determination of the practitioners! The experiences they offer are of the highest quality they can possibly manage, and they work hard to make the setting stimulating and varied. George goes out to play in the small fenced-off garden next to the church hall, joined by his key person, who pushes his friend Peter across the path in his buggy. The two boys then spend a very focused fifteen minutes watching ants coming and going across the path.

Eventually it is time for the pre-school and nursery children to tidy up and review their morning before going home, and for the reception children to wash their hands for lunch. The nursery children have built a very elaborate bus station, and reception class have completed their literacy and maths activities and spent some time on a variety of child-initiated activities. Each group of children sits down to review their morning with an adult before writing a To Do list for the next day or session.

As the reception children go back into class after lunch we go to watch the second group of nursery children arrive. They are greeted with music that will set the mood for the afternoon. We notice that the nursery is set up similarly to the morning session, but with a few differences. The afternoon group's To Do list from last week included a wish to discover more about sharks. One of the children had brought a leaflet into school on Friday from a trip to an aquarium, and an interest had been sparked. A table is therefore laid out with books about sharks, a selection of seashells and some pieces of natural sea sponge. A fish tank has been borrowed for the afternoon. Some fine felt pens and a selection of paper are laid out nearby for children to draw pictures.

The afternoon in the nursery turns out to be very different from the morning. When the children go outside, they ignore the bus conductor's hat in the box and the bus tickets. Instead, they put on pirates hats and build a shark from the bricks – one big enough to eat Jonah! They use the sponges to cool down the shark, which has become beached on the shore. Eventually, the shark is freed into the ocean without biting anyone too severely, and the children go inside to hear the story of Jonah and the whale. There is lots of excitement in this classroom!

We leave the nursery and go to visit reception class, who are having a busy afternoon. They start by doing a few minutes of maths to music, singing their numbers from one to 20. The class then gets changed into PE kit and goes into the hall to use the large climbing apparatus. The teacher reinforces body awareness and maths concepts through questioning. She encourages children to use their natural inclination to talk to themselves as they use mathematical language to describe their movements. Language use is encouraged throughout the session: there is no rule of silence in these lessons. The PE lesson is ended with the 'One, Two, Three' game. A few children hold numeral cards in different areas of the room. The teacher calls out a number and children have to skip, jump or hop towards the correct card. To make it trickier, the teacher then gives sums that the children have to answer before moving towards the numeral. On the way back to class and as they get dressed, again the children sing number songs and rhymes.

Once they are back into their school clothes, groups of children work on practical tasks involving lots of glue, plastic bottles, card and paint. The equipment that they need is organized so that they can work quite independently. In last week's literacy sessions, the teacher had introduced the author Richard Scarry. The class had been particularly inspired by his books about 'things that go', including vehicles that had little hope of ever going anywhere! This week the children can choose to be inventors. They put on 'Inventor' badges and set to work with a wide selection of materials including pulleys, ropes, guttering and wheels. This is where we meet Samantha, who has started to find the activity assigned to her group difficult.

Let's meet Samantha

Samantha's mother read numerous books about infant development when she was expecting Samantha. She was convinced that her baby recognized certain pieces of music and responded when they were played, and so she was not surprised to read that 20 weeks after conception, Samantha could hear in utero. Within an hour of her birth, Samantha preferred her mother's voice and would turn in response to it. Beverly Shirk, a paediatric nurse at Penn State Children's Hospital in the United States, recently studied the effects of recorded music versus the mother's voice upon sick children. Shirk and her team worked with 29 young children with critical illnesses. Either a recording of music, or one of the mother's voice with the music playing in the background was played to each child. The effect on each child's level of agitation was monitored. Shirk reported that: *'The children were most sedate when we used the therapeutic music combined with the mother's voice.'*[13]

Samantha's mother frequently sang to her before and after she was born, and constantly talked to her. When she did this, she was activating the connections between the neurons that are used for language. She was stimulating Samantha's brain to develop pathways used in pitch discrimination and later in identifying patterns of sound in the phonemic stage of reading. Unlike Kishan, Samantha speaks only English at home, and her brain is already running out of time to be really good at another language. The window of opportunity for learning a second language is from birth to the age of 12. The wisdom of an earlier start to language learning has been recognized by the government, with every child now having an entitlement to foreign language teaching in Key Stage 2.[14]

Samantha's neural development was different from that of the boys in her class, because she is a girl. Girls often demonstrate an early advantage with language acquisition. Samantha was a particularly early talker. By her first birthday she had a vocabulary of about 30 words, and from that point onwards her language acquisition was explosive. Her teacher recently read about the importance of encouraging children to 'pole-bridge'. Pole-bridging is when you mutter your thoughts aloud. Samantha's mother noticed that Samantha did this instinctively as a toddler, yet as she matured she became more aware

Turn to page 99 for more about pole-bridging.

of social etiquette, which doesn't encourage talking to oneself! Samantha's teacher encourages all the children to pole-bridge, and explains to their parents that this means that the child lays down even more neural connections. Connections become permanent only through regular revision, through practising the activity in the same way, practising it with some variations, and by adding language to the activity.

Samantha's parents were delighted that she was admitted to this school when they recently moved into the area. Samantha had attended a pre-school previously, where she had become confident and had made good all-round progress. She had then transferred to a nearby school where the practitioner favoured rote-learning. This type of teaching made Samantha feel anxious, which severely inhibited her learning. In situations of anxiety the body produces high levels of stress hormones. The hippocampus, which deals with memory, shuts down when the child feels stress. So at the end of a stressful lesson at that school Samantha would remember how she felt, but not what the practitioner had intended her to learn.

Fascinating Fact

Practitioners know that children who suffer from continual stress do not find learning easy. What they probably don't know is that the brains of these children have often become physically different from those of their more relaxed peers. Research on baboons has shown that stress can actually lead to shrinkage of the hippocampus.[15]

Fortunately, the practitioners in this setting understand the importance of creating a low-stress environment in order to maximize learning. Samantha benefits greatly from short yoga sessions, where she is developing calming and relaxation skills. Right now, Samantha is trying to fix a wheel onto her model car. Her teacher realizes that she is not finding it easy to stay on task, so puts the model aside until tomorrow and suggests that she goes outside to experiment with a ready-built car on the ramp. The classroom assistant helps her to verbalize her observations. When Samantha returns to the classroom, her teacher asks her to record her ideas on the class mind map with her group. Other children go outside to test their inventions and to use the big pulleys that the practitioners set up there at lunchtime. A few children have chosen to leave the activity to play elsewhere.

The afternoon in reception class continues with a sense of purposeful activity until eventually it is time to tidy up. This goes smoothly because the teacher uses familiar 'tidy-up music' to signal to the children that everybody should be busy helping. The children use simple charts to help them decide whether materials need to be thrown away or put into recycling boxes. Once the classroom is tidy, the teacher gives the children a choice of three

quiet activities while they listen to music and relax. She allows time to review the session and write Tuesday's To Do list. At the end of the day, children leave school clutching an assortment of books, certificates, notes and messages about their day. A number of children, including Samantha, have asked to borrow books by Richard Scarry from the book corner. They write their names on the 'Borrowers List' by the board. Celebration music can be heard from reception as the children put on their coats to go home. The nursery children leave to the sound of the song *Lifted* by Lighthouse Family. There is a relaxed atmosphere as some of the parents come into the classrooms to look at the To Do list and see their children's work.

After the children go home or to after school club, we leave the school feeling inspired to find out more about brain-based learning. What is the theory behind the many interesting things that we saw in action today? What research is there to back up the policies that the practitioners follow so enthusiastically? How did they start on their road to using these techniques? These are some of the questions that will be addressed in this book. The answers will hopefully help you to set out with confidence using brain-based learning techniques.

Plenary

Here are some points for reflection:

You read some questions that are amongst the most frequently asked by practitioners who want to find out about brain-based learning. How did you feel as you read the answers? What further questions might you like to ask?

We visited an early years setting where brain-based learning techniques are used. What aspects of their work seemed similar to those in your setting? What were the key differences? What were the three things on this visit that most interested you?

What did you think when you read the description of the brains of the fictitious children Carrie, George, Kishan and Samantha and their friends Peter and Madeline? They all come from enriched environments, yet their brains are all unique. Did the descriptions make you think of the learning behaviours of any of the children in your care?

Where do we go from here?

Introduction

We have hopefully answered some of your questions about brain-based learning and set the scene by our description of children in settings that use these techniques.

Part One

Now we will move on to consider the physical and emotional needs that must be addressed if children are to learn effectively.

Preparing the climate and context for learning

The Big Picture

In this section you will:

Step 1: Read about Maslow's 'hierarchy of needs' and consider how meeting these needs and creating a healthy setting affects children's learning

Step 2: Think about the philosophy behind inclusion and consider ways to find support while creating strong relationships with families and other agencies

Step 3: Learn about what Daniel Goleman calls 'emotional intelligence' and discover some ways to promote emotional literacy in your setting

Step 4: Consider the essential tools for learning and find out some new ways to foster strong self-esteem and the 'can-do' attitude in children

Step 5: Think about ways to manage children's behaviour positively and learn a new system for promoting desirable behaviours, called The Three As

Step 6: Read about the importance of good relationships between practitioners, parents and carers, consider the importance of attachment theory, and find out about different ways that practitioners have worked with the community

Step 1: Addressing children's physical needs

Maslow's hierarchy of needs

The psychologist Abraham Maslow (1908–1970) developed from his work with animals what he called 'a hierarchy of needs'. If you are tired and hungry, you choose to eat before going to sleep. If you are thirsty and hungry, you drink first: you instinctively tend to your most urgent need. These needs must be met in succession in order to optimize human performance. Lower order needs in the hierarchy have to be met before someone can advance to higher order functioning.

These layers extend beyond physiology. Think of a pyramid with each of these needs being a layer upon which the next can be laid. Without a strong foundation, the pinnacle cannot be built. The pinnacle is 'self-actualization', which in education we often describe as 'reaching full potential'.

These are the layers of the pyramid:

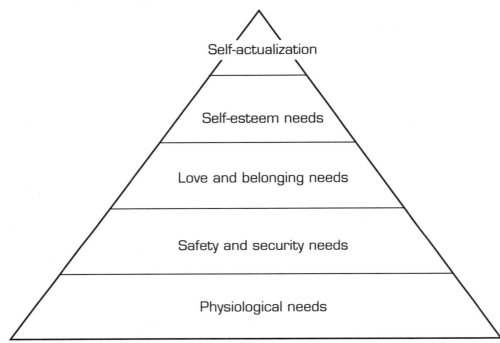

If a child is hungry, thirsty or tired, he will not be able to function. If he is worried about his safety, either at home or in the setting, and feels insecure, he will not function. If he does not build strong relationships or a sense of belonging, he will not move onto higher order functioning. If he has poor self-esteem, he will not believe in himself and his performance will be weak. It is our responsibility to ensure that, to the best of our ability, we provide for these hierarchical needs.

The physiological needs are the basis of the pyramid, and can be broken down into five areas: hydration, nutrition, sleep, movement, and attentional systems, which we will consider in turn.

Hydration

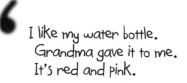

> I like my water bottle.
> Grandma gave it to me.
> It's red and pink.

Sarah, aged five

Children need to drink water throughout the day to remain hydrated, yet this basic physiological need is often ignored. Dehydration adversely affects the fluid-to-electrolyte balance in the body. For a child to be hydrated sufficiently the equivalent of eight to 12 small glasses of water should be consumed daily.

Fascinating Fact

Although the brain is only about 2.4 per cent of bodyweight it consumes up to 20 per cent of the body's energy. Enough water is needed to provide the appropriate electrolyte balance for optimal performance of the brain.

It is now a statutory requirement that in the EYFS, *'fresh drinking water must be available at all times'.*[16] This can be done by providing jugs of water for children to pour themselves, or by encouraging children to bring water bottles from home.

Nutrition

> *A healthy country would be one where health was not dictated by accident of birth and childhood experience. Everyone should have a fair chance of a long and healthy life.*

Department of Health, 1998.[17]

For optimum physical and intellectual development children need to be provided with a balanced diet. Hungry children can exhibit traits such as irritability or apathy. The chemicals that are primarily produced from food affect brain development and functioning. For example, research has highlighted the seriousness of iron deficiency on the developing brain. Iron is needed for myelination, the process by which the axons are coated with a greasy substance called myelin. Without adequate myelin, the communication between brain cells becomes sluggish. Iron deficiency in young children can lead to poor performance in problem solving and short-term memory activities.[18]

Fascinating Fact

It has been estimated that between 11 and 38 per cent of young children suffer from iron deficiency anemia in the UK.[19]

It is true that practitioners cannot control children's diets, but healthy eating is becoming a moral as well as a legal responsibility of settings. Part of our influence can be through controlling the foods that are offered, and part can be through educating children about healthy eating. Care also needs to be taken about when food is offered, as this can impact upon children's behaviour and their ability to learn. Researchers from the University of Virginia have found that the brain consumes glucose at a rate that depends upon the challenge of the task undertaken.[20] The researchers found that rats who were given glucose 30 minutes before tasks had superior performances in tests. The implication for practitioners is that attention needs to be paid to the provision of regular healthy snacks to nourish the brain as well as the body.

Fascinating Fact

Chewing on gum can improve mental performance. seventy-five people were divided into three groups: one group chewed gum, one chewed imaginary gum, and the third didn't chew at all. In memory tests, the chewers outperformed the non-chewers and the sham chewers.[21]

Sleep

In a study of sleep and behaviour problems among pre-schoolers, John V. Lavigne et al. described the relationship between amount of sleep and behaviour problems among pre-schoolers. Even when demographic variables were controlled, the relationship between less sleep at night and the presence of a psychiatric diagnosis was significant.[22]

George's mother was anxious to make sure that sleep was pleasant and comfortable for George. She was not willing to follow the 'cry it out' method to get him to sleep as a baby. The argument that this method 'works' was not enough to convince her that letting a baby cry himself to sleep is appropriate. We now know that the effect of long-term crying is increased levels of cortisol in the system. Cortisol is the hormone that is released during moments of stress. High levels of cortisol act as a block to normal functioning and learning, and can also negatively affect the immune system.

Researcher Christopher Coe took infant squirrel monkeys and separated them from their mothers, and then monitored their levels of 'distress calling' – that is, crying – and the cortisol levels in their blood. After a time, the monkeys ceased calling for their mothers and seemingly had overcome their distress. However, their cortisol levels remained high, and their immune systems and the development of their brains and other systems were negatively affected.[23]

Although sleep is something over which practitioners usually have little control, they can have some influence. They can plan topics about sleep and can give support to parents who are experiencing challenges with bedtime routines. They can also build in opportunities for relaxation during the day, and can vary the timetable so that the more challenging lessons are at children's most alert and receptive times.

Movement

> *If you are experienced, you will already know too well how energetic and physical young children are; their bodies are developing rapidly and they need to be active. It is actually painful for them at this stage of development to be still for long periods. Teaching methods should allow children to move imaginatively as well as to control and refine physical skills.*

Training Support Framework for the Foundation Stage, QCA, 2000

Young children are not designed to sit still for long periods. The best activities for learning are ones that require physical movement. Early years practitioners who demand that children sit for long periods to 'work' actually defeat their own aims. Getting up and moving around increases the oxygen in the blood stream and improves concentration. In addition, adding a movement or physical action to an activity aids children who are strong kinesthetic learners – plus it adds an element of fun!

Practitioners can help children to learn most effectively by planning for activities that allow for freedom of movement. They can limit the amount of sitting still and use plenty of brain breaks. They can incorporate actions into story and circle times and use music to accompany activities. They can also monitor individual children's activities to ensure that they receive a balance of different types of play.

Attentional systems

Early years practitioners know from experience that young children do not find it easy to concentrate for lengthy periods, especially when participating in adult-directed activities. A reasonable expectation is for children to focus for one minute for each year of their age, plus or minus one minute, depending on the individual child and the activity. Therefore five-year-olds might need a break from any one sustained activity every four to six minutes. This may mean just an opportunity for children to reflect and refocus, or to talk about what they are doing, or to change roles within a group, or to stretch or play a short game before continuing.

Children naturally experience high and low arousal cycles during the day. At certain times the blood flow to the brain increases and children are better at paying attention. Reception class teachers need to be mindful of the varied individual needs in their classes as they introduce the Literacy and Numeracy Strategies, and should consider how their timing impacts on the different highs and lows of attention in their class. The aim should be to sustain an optimal (not pre-determined or standard) time on task for each individual child, not to simply meet the demands of a paper curriculum. Practitioners can help children to learn to concentrate for longer periods by sitting and participating

We discuss the optimal time on task in more detail on page 92.

in activities, or organizing groups so that children with a longer concentration span play alongside the less mature children. They can also use affirmations such as, 'We are all good at reading quietly on the mat', or allow for a quiet time, or create an area where children can retreat if they feel tired.

Healthy settings

Among boys and girls aged 2–15, the proportion who were obese increased between 1995 and 2005, from 10.9 per cent in 1995 to 18.0 per cent in 2005 for boys and from 12.0 per cent to 18.1 per cent for girls.

Health Survey for England, 2005[24]

In spite of the advances of medicine and research into health in this new millennium, professionals are expressing increasing concern over the health of our children. Many factors have combined to create a generation that is increasingly dependent upon processed foods to eat, and technology for entertainment. Children are becoming increasingly sedentary, and statistics show that obesity is becoming a greater and greater problem in the Western world. In January 2008, the government published *Healthy Weight, Healthy Lives, a Cross-Government Strategy for England*, with an 'ambition to be the first major nation to reverse the rising tide of obesity and overweight in the population'.[25] The first target of this initiative is to reduce the number of obese and overweight children to the rates in the year 2000! This gives a sense of perspective to how the problem of obesity has been increasing exponentially.

Childhood diabetes, once a rare condition, is becoming increasingly common. The main risk factors for developing diabetes are family history and obesity. A study from the University of Bristol, tracking a population of people from 1985 to 2004, found a five-fold increase in the number of children under the age of five diagnosed with type 1 diabetes.[26]

There have been various responses to these concerns about the health of our children. Chef Jamie Oliver was thrust into the limelight when he undertook his *School Dinners* television programme. Jamie's challenge was to create menus for a Greenwich school that cost just 37 pence per meal. The result of Jamie's campaign, aside from making the 'Turkey Twizzler' a household name, was to create an outcry from the general public, which spurred the government to take action, and the School Food Trust was born.

Nutrition Based Standards are now statutory in UK schools, but more action is needed if the tide is to be turned. There are no easy answers. While Jamie's energy and outspokenness created a very public forum for discussion, practitioners are often faced with harsh realities. It can be frustrating to provide a healthy lunch for children and see them eat nothing, and then leave school with a bag of crisps in their hands! But no matter what the frustrations, it is imperative that we do our utmost to promote healthy living.

When drawing up a Food Policy, every aspect of food needs to be considered, including meals, packed lunches, snacks, cookery activities and 'treats'. It is wise to take regulations as a minimum and improve upon them. For example, try thinking about the messages given about food in the books that you read with children. It can be eye-opening to go through children's books looking for the subtle messages. A parent made the light-hearted observation that *'Cookie Monster seems to eat cookies all day with no repercussions for his health and as far as we know, no tooth decay!'* Another nursery teacher suddenly stopped herself mid-song as she sang a song about raindrops being 'lemon drops and gumdrops'.[27] Her habit had always been to invite suggestions from the children for more verses. The children would suggest foods which were invariably unhealthy. She made a new rule that every verse must contain at least one healthy food, such as 'carrots and ice-cream'. The children grew used to the new version and thought it fun. Singing songs and reading stories about sweets may seem innocent, and as an occasional event, it is. But at a time when the nation's health is seriously at risk, we need to be careful about every message that we give.

It is essential to be sensitive to economic and cultural differences and to individuals' personal beliefs. Sometimes it is necessary to keep in mind the adage 'more haste, less speed'. Education can go hand in hand with the liaison process. Recipes can be shared, lists of healthy packed lunch ideas can be made into booklets or sent out by email, and new foods can be introduced through snacks. In this time of financial challenge, families can be encouraged to share ideas for eating healthily on a tight budget. In one setting, parents led cooking 'workshops' where volunteers took turns teaching everyone how to make simple, economical dishes. These workshops turned into a popular event, drawing the community closer as they shared ideas, skills and good food.

The physical environment where children sit to eat can sometimes become one that is unsuited for healthy eating. While many settings provide calm, pleasant eating experiences, it can be more challenging for others to achieve this ideal. A noisy, hectic environment is not going to induce a sense of calm and wellbeing. A rigidly controlled, silent environment is equally unsuitable. Either of these environments results in stress, which causes levels of cortisol to rise. With creative thought, even in difficult situations, the negative aspects of mealtimes can be minimized. Tablecloths can be used to help soften noise, and rubber stoppers can be put on the legs of chairs to deaden sounds, and mealtimes can become more pleasant.

At a time when the number of children who eat a family meal is dwindling, practitioners can provide opportunities for children to experience the social aspects of sharing food. Research consistently shows a link between eating family meals and wellbeing in children. For example, University of Minnesota researchers discovered that girls who ate regular family meals were less likely to develop eating disorders.[28] Other studies have shown that children who eat regular family meals tend to have greater academic and social success. Of course, we cannot predict how the young children in our care will turn out, but by giving frequent opportunities for them to experience family style eating, we are providing some small measure of immunity against disorders while aiding social and emotional growth.

The recent health crisis has led to statutory requirements for the provision of healthy foods, and traditional cooking projects have made way for healthier alternatives. Cooking projects do not need to involve the oven. Making sandwiches with wholemeal bread and healthy fillings, or mixing ingredients to make dips and cutting vegetables to accompany them, are all great activities for cookery projects. Healthy soups or wholewheat pasta dishes can be made with children's help, such as weighing, counting, then cutting up vegetables with child-safe knives and mixing the ingredients in the saucepan before cooking. Children can be introduced to foods that they have never tried, and healthy eating habits can be supported.

The first outcome of *Every Child Matters* is 'be healthy', and settings and schools are held increasingly accountable for the ways in which they support and promote healthy living.[29] The other four *Every Child Matters* outcomes are to a large extent dependent upon health, as it is far more difficult to enjoy your life and achieve to your full potential if you are not healthy. We can no longer afford to take children's health for granted, even in the most privileged social areas. Our battle is no longer simply against malnourishment or poor medical provision – it is against the very culture of the twenty-first century.

Alongside poor diet, many children have a startlingly poor attitude towards play and exercise. Most young children have a natural desire to be active, but they need to maintain these healthy attitudes. This is one area in which early years settings tend to have more success than school settings. However, we have no room to be complacent. Academic pressures can lead to children being given less time to be out of doors, and the pressures from society can lead to them being more sedentary at home. Creative solutions need to be found that gently move indoor children out of doors. Taking indoor games outdoors, playing games such as hopscotch alongside the children, or teaching skipping rhymes can help the reticent child to become more active.

Attention also needs to be paid to getting toddlers and babies out of doors. Thankfully, there is now a requirement in the EYFS that all children should spend time playing out of doors every day. This means that even in pre-schools or pack-away settings with limited access to outdoor provision, practitioners must plan for outdoor activities every day for all ages. Babies and young children can visit the park, a local playing field or even a town garden for this outdoor activity, but it must now happen every day.

In this age of working parents, technology in the home, and a fear of the dangers of being outside, many children have a very limited experience of the outdoors. For some children, the practitioner may be the only person who can open their eyes to the pleasures of an active lifestyle. Many babies have never been in a pram under a tree watching the leaves, clouds and birds. Many children have never pulled on wellington boots and walked in the woods. There is as much value in planning outings where children simply kick through leaves, jump in puddles, or build a fort out of fallen branches as there is in visits to museums. For young children, a walk through the handful of trees at the back of the park, stopping to look at bugs, leaves and cobwebs can become an amazing outdoor forest adventure!

The twenty-first century is a very different place from even the end of the twentieth century, and there are many new challenges facing us. While medicine and healthcare have improved in many ways, the health of the population has declined. An increasing responsibility for instilling healthy habits now falls upon schools and settings. This work needs to be undertaken with a clear sense of purpose, because the wellbeing of future generations depends upon it.

Step 2: Inclusion

Much more than a policy requirement, inclusion is founded upon a moral position which values and respects every individual and which welcomes diversity as a rich learning resource.

Centre for Studies on Inclusive Education[30]

The mix of children in many settings has changed over recent years as legislation has been passed making it unlawful to discriminate against disabled children when providing any service, including education. The general view of the rights of individuals in terms of equal opportunities and inclusion in society has evolved to a point that inclusion has come to be seen as desirable and just. The government has made it clear that the five outcomes of *Every Child Matters* apply to all children. Yet inclusion is far more than simply a matter of policy. It is a fundamental shift in attitudes and thinking. Not only are settings expected to accommodate children from a far wider range of backgrounds, but at last they are also doing so in a way that celebrates differences and diversity.

As we move well into the new millennium, in any one setting there are likely to be children with very diverse backgrounds and needs, such as children whose families are refugees, migrant workers, or travellers; children who are cared-for; children with little or no understanding of English; and children with physical, emotional or behavioural difficulties. Demands have increased upon practitioners to understand the needs of these different groups of children. This is not always an easy task, but it is one that offers great rewards as we move towards a more inclusive society.

Along with this shift towards catering for more children in mainstream settings has come an increased effort to coordinate agencies so that families receive focused services. When accommodating a child with special needs, it is essential to work from the understanding that you should not be working in isolation. This is clearly the aim of the government:

> Getting everyone, families and professionals, working effectively together at the earliest opportunity is vital for parents with a young disabled child.

The Rt. Hon. Gordon Brown, Prime Minister

The government has shown its commitment to this inclusive society by initiatives such as Early Support. Strong relationships need to be built between different agencies, which can take hard work and perseverance, but the rewards are immeasurable.

The emergence of this new age of inclusion is timely, as the proportion of children with some types of special needs has been increasing dramatically over the past decade. It is now estimated that about 7 per cent of children are disabled.[31] The number of children with autistic spectrum disorders is rising at an astonishing rate. Prior to the 1990s, researchers estimated four to five cases of autism in every 10,000 people. The National Autistic Society now estimates that there is a prevalence rate of about 1 in 100 children.[32] Numbers of children with attention disorders are also sharply rising. The statistics for the prevalence of attention disorders vary due to the difficulty in obtaining clear diagnoses, but the numbers of children with attention disorders quoted in research now range from 2 per cent to as high as 18 per cent.

There are many theories about this ongoing increase in statistics, with professionals, parents and researchers disagreeing, often very passionately, on the causes. Some experts believe that there has simply been an improvement in the methods of diagnosis, although the evidence suggests that this cannot be the only reason for the higher figures being reported year upon year. Others hypothesize that the better survival rates of premature babies contribute at least some small percentage. There is a groundswell of parents and professionals who blame childhood vaccines or other aspects of modern life. Certainly, the lifestyle of today's young children is vastly different from that of their parents and grandparents. Diets have changed, often for the worse. Food additives and preservatives have become so commonplace that it can take 15 minutes – and a magnifying glass – to decipher the ingredients list on a simple loaf of bread. Children eat from plastic plates, drink from plastic beakers and suck on plastic toys before they can walk. One scare after another about contaminants in children's toys hits the headlines. While mercury has now been removed from vaccinations, ingredients such as aluminium and formaldehyde – otherwise known as antifreeze – are still present.

With research projects being largely funded by the drug companies who have a vested interest in having their products deemed safe, government policies focused on attempting to eradicate childhood diseases, and changing expectations for how children should behave in school, it becomes almost impossible to come to a reasonable conclusion about the causes of this modern phenomenon. Most likely, it is a combination of all these factors, but whatever the reasons, practitioners have to familiarize themselves with the needs of children with a far wider range of challenges than in the past.

Yet the fundamental philosophy of inclusion lies much deeper than simply ensuring that all children with special needs have access to services. On the *Ask the Experts* page of the DCFS website, *Inclusion*, John Galloway describes this change of focus that goes far further than legislation:

> *Overall the view of what "inclusion" is seems to have matured and become more inclusive. The notion of "personalisation" is more strongly promoted, so that inclusion has shifted from being focused on SEN to being about learning needs and curriculum relevance for all pupils.*[33]

Personalized learning is the key for truly embracing inclusion. This means that the curriculum needs to be child-led, not simply tweaked or adapted for children who fall at the outer edges of a normal curve. One of the keys to success is finding resources within the special needs community to create a greater understanding of the child's needs. Many practitioners find that it helps to take a staff meeting to do this research. Others ask the child's parent, social worker, health visitor or another expert for input. By making information available to everyone, practitioners can support one another in their learning.

Inclusion is most likely to be successful in settings where involvement is sought from all practitioners, managers, committee members, governors, volunteers, parents, carers and relevant outside agencies. Partnership with parents is essential for the successful care of any child, but it is even more so for those children with special needs. Parents can be the source of information in addition to being the person who best understands the uniqueness of their child. It is important to recognize the emotional significance of inclusion for many families. One mother described inclusion like this:

> *Having my child accepted into nursery school made me think of a game I used to play with my friends. We would jump over and back an imaginary boundary and, in our game, the pocket lint in our pockets would turn to gold, and back again. Nursery school was a place where our pocket lint was gold rather than pocket lint. A place where our family made sense and we felt at home.*

Sadly, for many families, the setting is one of the few places where they do feel at home. They have often experienced exclusion. Different people respond to this in different ways, with some being open and ready to work in partnership, but others feeling defensive and protective of their child. Some relationships take a little more time and work than others. Practical measures can help with building trust. It is vital that you listen carefully to parents' concerns. Finding time at the start and end of the session to speak directly with the parent or carer is important – although, of course, you should avoid discussing sensitive issues in front of children. If you cannot answer a question fully, make an agreement about when you will talk. Some parents appreciate regular phone calls or emails. Ask parents what their preference is for communication, and then 'go the extra mile'. One father was thrilled that his day care provider emailed him a photograph of his daughter riding on the tricycles for the first time. Attention to details and sharing small, everyday achievements with parents helps to build confidence and trust.

With the increasing numbers of children with diverse needs in the early years, there has been an increase in the number of official and more casual support groups. In addition to personal relationships with other professionals, many practitioners find invaluable resources on the internet, where they find information and a space for discussion and support from other practitioners and experts. One such example is the Foundation Stage Forum.[34] On this discussion board, practitioners discuss the philosophical aspects of their work alongside giving practical advice on many subjects.

Practitioners also need to be sensitive to the needs of parents when their child may have a rare condition, a combination of different needs, or an unfamiliar syndrome. These parents may benefit from advice on where to go for professional support, resources, or contact with other families who face similar challenges. A network of contacts within the local community may support parents who might be feeling uncertain, threatened, insecure, or even guilty about the needs of their child.

An inclusion policy, however, is more than the practical considerations for accommodating specific individual children. Inclusion demands critical, honest consideration of culture, policies and practices. Simple assumptions about cultural norms can act as barriers for families whose lives do not fit that 'norm'. By contrast, considering those families and building in traditions that celebrate their lives and differences can open up avenues of communication and learning.

It is essential to ensure that different groups are represented without discrimination in materials such as posters, toys and books. This does not mean simply buying books about children with disabilities and special needs. It means looking really critically at materials and ensuring that they include children naturally, as if they have the right to be in society. There is a growing awareness that disabled children have often been 'invisible' in published materials. A recent project called *In the Picture* aims to persuade publishers to automatically include disabled children in children's books. Renowned children's illustrator Quentin Blake has supported the project, saying, '*it is about disabled children being part of the make-up of the story, in the swimming pool or playground, or wherever*'.[35]

If we extend the concept further than that of picture books, inclusion is about all children being a part of not just story books, but a part of every real-life childhood experience, both within our settings and schools and in our communities.

Step 3: **Developing emotional intelligence**

What is emotional intelligence?

> *There is perhaps no psychological skill more fundamental than resisting impulse. It is the root of all emotional self-control, since all emotions, by their very nature, lead to one or another impulse to act.*

Daniel Goleman[36]

In his book *Emotional Intelligence: Why it can matter more than IQ*, Daniel Goleman argues that emotional intelligence can prove to be a more significant factor in a child's future than any other measure of intelligence. Goleman quotes the research done in the 1960s by psychologist Walter Mischel at Stanford University. A group of four-year-olds were offered a marshmallow as a treat. If they were willing to wait for the adult to run an errand, they would be allowed two marshmallows when he returned:

Some four-year-olds were able to wait what must surely have seemed an endless 15 to 20 minutes for the experimenter to return. To sustain themselves in their struggle they covered their eyes so they wouldn't have to stare at temptation, or rested their heads in their arms, talked to themselves, sang, played games with their hands and feet, even tried to go to sleep. These plucky pre-schoolers got the two-marshmallow reward. But others, more impulsive, grabbed the one marshmallow, almost always within seconds of the experimenter's leaving the room on his 'errand'.

These four-year-olds were tracked down as they were graduating from high school:

The emotional and social difference between the grab-the-marshmallow preschoolers and their gratification-delaying peers was dramatic. Those who had resisted temptation at four were now, as adolescents, more socially competent: personally effective, self-assertive, and better able to cope with the frustrations of life.

One of the greatest challenges for the parent and practitioner is helping children to learn to manage their emotions. Indeed, impulsivity seems often to be synonymous with early years! You can help children to learn to manage impulsivity through circle time activities with a 'what if' scenario, playing games that involve waiting and turn-taking, and exploring emotions and behaviour through stories, role play and fantasy games.

Daniel Goleman identifies the five aspects of emotional literacy as:

 self-awareness

 management of emotions

 self motivation

 handling relationships

 empathy

Practitioners are becoming increasingly familiar with these categories as they use various social skills resources such as the SEAL (Social and Emotional Aspects of Learning) programme, which has been developed around these emotional intelligence domains.[37] Developing skills in each of these five areas is essential if children are to achieve the *Every Child Matters* outcomes.

Developing self-awareness and managing emotions

The key to helping children to develop self-awareness and mood management is to recognize and give labels to the emotions that they are feeling. Kishan's teacher often does this. 'You look frustrated, Kishan,' she says, when she sees him about to smash a Lego® model because he doesn't have enough pieces to make it stand upright. Kishan stops for a moment to reflect. 'I bet you're annoyed that the model keeps falling over. I would be annoyed too! Now, I wonder what we can do to get it to stand up. Who do you think might have some good ideas to help you?'

The situation for Kishan is defused. He has a label for how he felt. He is reassured that his teacher would also have felt frustrated in his situation. He absorbs the message that it's OK to feel frustrated, and that there are ways to deal with the emotion. Some of the other children give him their bricks and help him to build a base for his model. Later, at story time, his teacher refers to his struggle with the Lego® model. She reads the story of 'Titch' to the class. 'How do you think Titch felt when his brother and sister always took the best stuff?' she asks. 'Angry,' says one child. 'Sad,' says another. 'I bet he was frustrated,' says Kishan, remembering the label that his teacher had given his feelings earlier. 'Yes!' agrees the teacher, and proceeds to talk about what Titch could do to deal with his feelings.

Self-motivation

Children are born with the strong desire to learn. They do not need extrinsic motivators to persuade them to explore their world – it is instinctive to them. This intrinsic motivation usually lasts through the toddler stages into the early years. By primary age, there is a subtle change in expectations about children's learning. Even when experts talk about enthusiasm for learning, they tend to talk about *creating* motivation, as opposed to fostering that very motivation that children are born with:

> *Every teacher knows that truly effective learning and teaching focuses on individual children, their strengths, their needs, and the approaches which engage, motivate and inspire them.*

Excellence and Enjoyment: A Strategy for Primary Schools, 2003

Research shows that as children progress through the education system, their self-motivation declines as their dependence on extrinsic motivators increases. Sadly, in the early years this transition is sometimes already being made, as children begin to seek extrinsic rewards such as stickers or smiley faces for doing the very activities that at one time would have satisfied them. Ironically, studies show that the offering of rewards actually does not work, as pointed out by author Alfie Kohn:

> *Children and adults alike are less successful at many tasks when they're offered a reward for doing them – or for doing them well.*[38]

Luckily for our four children, the practitioners in their settings understand that most of the children have a natural drive to learn that has not been tarnished by an emphasis on extrinsic motivators. They understand that children learn best when their curiosity is engaged, when they share ownership of what is being taught and learned, and when the level of challenge is appropriate to individual needs.

Handling relationships and developing empathy

Research suggests that the school drop-out rate is between two and eight times greater for children who are rejected by their peers than for those who have friends. Many children who become 'rejects' socially are those who have not learned the skills of being able to read the emotional cues of others. There have been shown to be connections between the social skills of children at the age of seven and the incidence of mental health problems in later life.

Studies have shown that providing opportunities for children to engage in activities such as drama can measurably increase children's social skills. A report in *Psychological Science* in 2004 describes how a Canadian study of how music affects IQ turned up some additional, surprising results. The children were divided into four groups. Two groups were given music instruction, and of the two control groups, one was given drama instruction and one given no instruction. The researchers found that:

Unexpectedly, children in the drama group exhibited substantial pre-to-post-test improvements in adaptive social behavior that were not evident in the music groups.[39]

This finding confirms the importance of making plenty of time for activities such as drama which can so easily become squeezed out by other curriculum demands.

Drama can be built into story or circle time. One practitioner asked half her group of children to pretend to be Cinderella and the other half to pretend to be the Ugly Sisters. The children were asked to describe how they felt and suggest ways that the two characters could resolve their differences. During singing activities, she asked the children to sing familiar songs in different voices, ranging from emotions such as, 'sad voice' or 'scared voice', to crazy voices that would crack the children up, such as 'dog's voice' or 'alien's voice'. The purpose was to get the children to consciously explore how it feels to demonstrate different emotions and to put a label to those feelings.

Helping young children to build good relationships and develop empathy is sometimes a challenge. Some children do just seem to have better interpersonal skills than others. Howard Gardner identifies these skills as an individual 'intelligence' in his work on the multiple intelligences. An emphasis on cooperation in the early years setting will lead to better interpersonal skills between children. Kishan sometimes needs help with his friendships. He is always enthusiastic and finds it difficult to think through an action in preparation for an event. This can lead him into conflict with his peers.

We discuss the multiple intelligences on pages 139–43

Kishan's teacher encourages his enthusiasm but will step in to help him manage conflict. Sometimes Kishan needs to role-play what he plans to do, before he does it. His teacher takes the time to kneel so that she can gain strong eye contact. She draws Kishan's attention to the cues of other children and keeps her comments short and simple: 'John pushed your hand away. John didn't like you taking the brick from him.' By being explicit, his teacher is helping him to learn to read the cues of others and develop interpersonal skills. He is developing emotional intelligence.

Developing the right mindset

Researcher Carol Dweck from Stanford University in California takes the concept of emotional intelligence and adds what she calls 'another dimension', by identifying what she calls two different 'mindsets'.[40] These mindsets, Dweck believes, define how we live our lives and ultimately whether or not we fulfil our potential. The two mindsets are the 'fixed mindset' and the 'growth mindset'. People with a fixed mindset believe that there are limits to what they can achieve. They focus on proving themselves to be smart or superior rather than putting their energy into improving their performance. People with a growth mindset believe that they can learn and develop, and that intelligence and talent are not fixed phenomena.

If children develop a fixed mindset, they grow up lacking the skills and attitudes needed to overcome failure. They do not just experience failure – they let it define them. Therefore, if an attempt to climb the rope ladder fails, the child becomes in her own mind, 'the kid who can't climb the rope ladder'. Instead of learning from failure, the child identifies personally with the failure and *becomes* the failure. A child with a growth mindset sees failure as something to be overcome. She is 'the kid who can't climb the rope ladder *yet*'. This does not mean that she will like failing, and she might show all the normal signs of frustration. She might need help to manage the emotions that go along with failure. But she will be open to trying again.

Often the child's mindset will be already in place when she enters pre-school. Thankfully, mindsets can change, especially when children are young. The language that you use with children will influence the development of mindsets. As children experience frustration and failure, use phrases such as, 'Yesterday you managed two steps – today you managed four! I wonder how many you will do by the end of the week?' Purposely use the word 'yet', such as, 'Oh, I see that you can't hammer the nails all the way yet.' Make observations such as, 'Look – the nail is showing through this end of the wood now.' Help her to recognize improvement, and make it clear that you fully expect her to learn to hammer effectively in time. Avoid making comments such as, 'You are such a great hammerer', which suggest that hammering is an innate talent!

It is also very important to model perseverance. Children can view adults as superheroes, and it is important to show them that even adults have more to learn. For example, George's key person was baking with a group of children but couldn't get the consistency of her mixture correct. 'It won't roll out,' she mused, 'but when we add water it gets sticky.' Then she turned the problem over to the children, 'What do you think we should do?'

'Let's ask Chanda,' suggested George, 'she's a *good* cook!'

'Yes she is!' laughed his key person, calling to Chanda, who came over to help. The children learned how to handle the dough, but most importantly, they learned that even their most admired adults have to sometimes ask for help.

On a professional level, we can influence the ethos of our workplace by ensuring that we take a 'growth' outlook towards our professional development. We need to believe in our own abilities, while still taking risks and learning more. This will have an impact upon the atmosphere and ethos of the setting. Dweck points out that having a growth mindset is our responsibility:

> *As parents, teachers, and coaches, we are entrusted with people's lives. They are our responsibility and our legacy, we now know that the growth mindset has a key role to play in helping us fulfill our mission and in helping them fulfill their potential.*

Step 4: Providing children with the tools for learning

Fostering strong self-esteem

> *Babies and children become independent by being able to depend upon adults for reassurance and comfort.*

Early Years Foundation Stage, 2008

At home Carrie continually receives positive feedback. Her mother held her for long periods as a newborn, ignoring those who said that she was spoiling her baby. Instinctively she spoke the secret language of 'motherese' to Carrie, and she encouraged Carrie to begin to explore her world with confidence.

A baby is quick to develop responses to external stimuli, and the parent plays a part in shaping this pattern of responses. Children's personality development is, in part, a reflection of what they have learned in their first three or four years. So as the child enters the early years setting, there is a personality shaped by the interactions that she has experienced so far. This could be positive, or it could be negative and inhibit the child's learning. Carrie's experiences have so far been positive. She knows that she is clever and capable, and kind and gentle. She is confident and receptive to learning.

Let us consider again Maslow's hierarchy of needs. Once a child's physiological, security and social needs are provided for, the next layer of the pyramid can be laid: that of self-esteem. Maslow divided the esteem needs again into two layers, a lower one and a higher one. At the lower level is the need for the respect of others. At the higher level is respect for oneself.

If a child feels respected by others, then the need for self-respect can be met. Yet sadly, most of us can recall one or more specific incidents in our childhood that affected our self-esteem for the worse. Thoughtless comments can affect children for a lifetime. One practitioner shared her story about how she had never learned to swim because of an experience some thirty years in her past:

One day, when I was five or six, we were having a family day at the beach. I was quite happy body-surfing in the waves, when my uncle came over and offered to take me in deeper.

Although I was a bit nervous, he took me in deeper and deeper, and then let me go when a big wave approached. I managed to surf it for a few yards, then was tossed under.

I came up coughing and spluttering. It was probably only a few seconds before my uncle grabbed me, and had he given me some reassurance I would have had another go. But instead, he carried me into the shallow water and told me, 'You stay here, girl, where it's safe. I didn't realize you were too big to float.'

I never ventured out of my depth from that day onwards.

Imagine that each child in your care has pockets in his clothing in which he contains his self-esteem. A negative experience makes a hole in the pockets, allowing the contents to leak out, eventually leaving the child's pockets empty. After a while, the obstacles that face him on the pathway of learning might seem too daunting and his progress could be slowed or even halted. Conversely, positive experiences will help him to fill his pockets with useful attitudes and tools for his learning adventures. Positive self-esteem is one of the greatest gifts that can be given to a child. An early years setting where positive relationships are fostered ensures that children experience success. Each child then loads his or her self-esteem pockets with useful tools for learning. When a child experiences the constant respect of others, without the hindrance of unnecessary praise or harsh criticism, he can then develop what Maslow described as the higher level of self-esteem, which is self-respect.

Consider the difference between these two responses – both positive – by a practitioner who notices that Samantha has built an interesting model from the Duplo®:

Response 1: 'That's a great model! Well done! Can you tidy up for lunch now?'

Response 2: 'Samantha, that's an interesting model. I notice that you used just the red and blue bricks. Why did you choose those colours?'

The second response not only leads Samantha into further learning, but it also gives her some positive feedback about herself. It shows that the practitioner has really looked at the model and has thought about what she has done. It shows that her work is worthwhile and has been valued, but it is not empty praise, which would lead to Samantha seeking approval rather than focusing on the process. This sort of experience helps Samantha to maintain strong self-esteem. The most effective practitioners aim to use only positive language in their settings. A good rule is the 'four-to-one' rule, where four pieces of positive language should be used for each neutral one.

Approval or disapproval is also exhibited through body language. Children are extremely adept at reading non-verbal cues, which can be used to support healthy self-esteem. There is no need to create a frantic atmosphere of high-energy tricks for giving approval, but a well-timed round of applause, a hug, a thumbs-up, a wink, or a pat on the back are all ways to give feedback without using words. It is important to be sensitive to the fact that children have different 'currencies' for communication, with some preferring an energetic celebration and others being happier with eye-contact and a smile. Children can also develop their own systems for giving and receiving feedback. One reception class developed a ritual of giving each other high-fives, to a rhyme:

'Five up high

Five down low,

Ten in the air

And away you go!'

> Mrs Woods gives me the thumbs-up when I do good listening. I give her the thumbs-up too. It makes us laugh.

Seth, aged five

You may sometimes need to make a special effort to boost the self-esteem of individual children. This might be an individual programme where all staff in the setting work to give the child explicit positive messages about herself. The activities for these children need to be planned to ensure that they experience regular success and receive support when the task is challenging, as any small event that these children perceive as 'failure' can diminish their self-esteem. Circle time is a powerful way of supporting self-esteem, and this is what we are going to consider next.

Circle time for supporting self-esteem

> Circle time is fun. My teachers sit on the floor too, but they are a bit old so they get stiff.

Samir, aged four

> *Circle Time provides the ideal group listening system for enhancing children's self-esteem, promoting moral values, building a sense of team and developing social skills. It is a democratic system, involving all children and giving them equal rights and opportunities.*

Jenny Mosley[41]

Circle time is one of the most practical tools for promoting self-esteem in young children. Each person comes to circle time with unconditional acceptance. Circle time is not a place for judgement or discipline measures. It is true that many practitioners find that discipline becomes easier and children's behaviour is seen to improve when a good circle time programme is put into place, but this is a side effect rather than an objective. Many practitioners incorporate activities from the SEAL programme, which has an objective of *'using teaching methods that are participative and experiential rather than didactic'*, into their regular circle times.[42] Many settings introduce circle time as soon as the children can sit in the circle for a few minutes, listen while other children speak, and begin to contribute to the group. Some children are ready for this at around three years old, whereas others will not be ready until later. Circle time is about sharing and reinforcing kindness, teamwork and positive attitudes; circle time reinforces positive self-images. Sessions should be short and focused.

One nursery nurse called circle time 'Sam Time', after the soft toy dog she used as a 'speaking object'. The speaking object is the object that a child holds when it is his or her turn to speak. She found that circle time was easier to manage once the children understood two simple rules. First, nobody was allowed to interrupt the speaker, including herself. Second, children were only to say positive, kind or thoughtful things about other people. Laying down these basic principles helps circle time to go smoothly and achieve its goals.

After a warm up time, such as 'Pass on a smile', where the practitioner smiles at the first child who smiles, turns to the next child and passes the smile along, a wide variety of activities can follow. Some will actively promote positive self-esteem, for example 'Pass the speaking object', where the speaking object is passed around the circle. The children can speak when they are holding it about a topic such as 'What I did outside today', 'My best achievement this week', or 'What a friend did to help me'.

At circle time, children can revisit difficult situations and find solutions to problems.

They can be given opportunities to express their feelings and develop empathy for others. Children's successes can be celebrated and their individual achievements can be recognized. They can be given opportunities to ask and to answer questions within the safety of the circle, and can give and receive feedback. In these ways, circle time fosters self-esteem and emotional intelligence, which we now know are a greater indicator of future success and happiness than intellectual achievement.

The essential attitudes for effective learning

> *When the emotions are brought into dynamic equilibrium with reason, insight, action and even survival, learning becomes a rational, creative process.*

Carla Hannaford[43]

A child will not attain the early learning goals if she does not have the attitudes that are essential for meaningful learning. These attitudes are the tools that the child loads into her self-esteem pockets and uses as she encounters challenges. Whereas skills can be directly demonstrated, taught and practised, attitudes have to be fostered. This calls for keen observation skills on the part of the practitioner. It is important to consider the attitude that the child has towards each activity. If her attitude is positive, she will be able to improve on her performance. If her attitude is negative, her performance will probably be weak and the likelihood is that next time she will repeat the poor performance rather than strive to improve and learn more.

It is as important to acknowledge the children's attitudes as it is to acknowledge their achievements. For example, when the nursery nurse in Samantha's class noticed that Samantha had sorted all the dolls' clothes according to type and size, she commented on the way that Samantha had undertaken the activity. 'Samantha, I noticed how tricky it was for you to decide what to do with the dolls' dresses. You stuck at the job instead of giving up – thank you!'

The child with a full set of tools for learning is:

 Enthusiastic

 Imaginative

 Cooperative

 Thoughtful

 Confident

 Responsible

 Creative

 Deliberate

Empathetic

 Resourceful

 Persistent

 Purposeful

 Determined

 Humorous

 Resilient

A child with these tools has enthusiasm for all the experiences that the early years can offer. He can cooperate in a group and contribute confidently. He may have preferences for certain types of activities, and these preferences may alter according to his needs, but he is keen to participate and he is creative and imaginative in his play. Yet he also thinks before he acts – he has emotional intelligence and he can delay gratification and consider the possible consequences of his actions before acting. He takes responsibility for his actions and is deliberate in his thought processes.

This child has empathy and can see issues from different perspectives. He is versatile and can adapt to new challenges. When faced with a challenge, he is resilient. He does not blame others or himself for failure – instead, he has coping strategies and sees failure as a part of the learning challenge. He is resourceful and knows how to seek help when he needs it. His learning is purposeful. And if all else fails, he has a sense of humour that will carry him through!

Our four children, George, Carrie, Kishan and Samantha, have different combinations of these attributes in varying levels. It is the job of the adults who care for them to help them to build upon these. No two children are the same, and each child's profile will develop and alter according to his experiences and stage of development. When a child has a full set of these attributes, he will have a strong 'can-do' attitude, which is one of the greatest gifts that you can give the children in your care.

We can do it!

Children with strong self-esteem have what could be called a 'can-do' attitude. This 'can-do' attitude needs to be fostered in the early years, as it lays the foundations for positive learning attitudes in later life. This is equally important across all areas, from social and personal skills to physical and intellectual development. It is as important that a child believes that she can speak aloud in circle time as it is that she feels that she can dress herself, wash her hands, or learn to read independently. The key to successful learning is for the child to have the skills for success along with a strong self-belief that she will succeed.

George sometimes needs adult support when he encounters a challenge. For example, when he sat to thread some beads in the maths area, he found the activity challenging. An adult sat down at the table and helped him. After a while, George discovered that if he held the beads firmly on the table, he could manage the threading independently. His self-esteem was boosted as he experienced success. If he frequently receives support in this way, he will become more persistent.

In George's pre-school the adults often discuss ways to help the children become more independent. The pre-school is in shared accommodation, and everything has to be packed up after each session. In spite of this, the practitioners have made many adjustments to the room that help children to do things for themselves. The coat pegs are fixed at a lower height, so that children can hang up and fetch their own coats; boxes and shelves are clearly labelled to help children with making choices; drinks are set out on a low table, so that children can help themselves; and there is a step stool in the bathroom so that children can wash their own hands. Children with additional needs are carefully monitored to ensure they are as independent as possible, by providing physical support or adaptations of furniture, routines and resources. The adults encourage children to plan their own time and to select and put away the equipment as they need it. The practitioners are also careful to ensure that they model the 'can-do' attitude themselves. For example, when a new go-cart was delivered in pieces in a big box, the practitioners gathered the tools that they needed and built the go-cart with the children. Photographs were then used to make a book about the activity.

Practitioners need to work to ensure that children also develop a 'can-do' attitude to literacy: all children should believe that they are readers and writers, no matter what their stage of literacy development. Opportunities should be given for children to write for a purpose, such as writing shopping lists, letters to Grandma, signs, labels and reminder notes. Writing materials should also be provided for children to use in role-play activities both indoors and outside. For example, in one reception class the children helped to convert their home corner into a garden centre. They made labels and price tags, wrote out receipts for customers, and put up signs about how to care for the plants.

Even from the earliest stages of mark making, it is important to encourage children to believe that they are writing. A childminder spoke of her amazement when she saw her youngest child imitate the older children when using chalks on the patio outside:

> *The four-year-olds that I look after were drawing on the patio. They would attempt to write their names near to their drawings, saying the letters aloud as they did so. Mia, who is only eighteen-months-old, was following them, making little marks on the floor with a chalk from the box. She was muttering to herself, saying "Mia" as she made each mark. She was acting like a writer even though her "writing" was only tiny little dashes on the patio.*

In Samantha's class, some children write pages of what might appear to be scribble, yet when they 'read' it aloud it contains elaborate sentences to make up a story. Other children have advanced further, and their writing contains a variety of symbols running from left to right on the page. Other children have advanced even further and include some letters and numbers in their writing. A few children include some c-v-c (consonant-vowel-consonant) words and their writing is demarcated into clear words and sentences. This is a normal range in any early years setting, but the point is that all the children are writers. You don't have to be able to spell to be able to write!

Similarly, you don't have to know phonics to be able to read. How many times have you heard a parent say, 'But she can't read – she just uses her memory'? This important stage of reading, where the child memorizes a favourite book and 'reads' it over and over again, needs to be actively encouraged. In addition to learning to recognize the words that she is 'reading' and how stories work, the child is learning a much more important lesson – the 'can-do' lesson that she can read!

In one classroom children worked in the book-making area, illustrating and binding their own books. A wide variety of materials was available: card, paper, scissors, glue, Sellotape, treasury tags, paper clips, hole punches and so on. Some ready-made books were available for children to take and fill in with pictures and their own writing. Other children would organize their own paper and card and bring their completed books to the practitioner for her to bind them on the spiral binder. These home-made books were displayed in the book corner and on the table by the parents' notice board.

Another reception teacher devised a system to help the children in her class who were reluctant writers:

'*Several of the children in my class would frequently interrupt my classroom assistant or me to ask for spellings, or to ask one of us to scribe for them. They just didn't believe that they could write independently. So we set up systems for different types of writing.*

Sometimes we use wordbooks, where they have to "have a go" on one side of the page before asking an adult to check their attempt. Other times they can come to ask me to scribe for them, but when they have a green book, green paper, or green pencils on their desk, it means, "Green is for Go, Go Go!" They then are expected to write independently and not ask for help until they have finished the task.

Somehow this relieves the pressure for them and they are happy to have a go, meaning that the adults can work with other children. We love our "Green is for Go" times!'

A setting that is organized for the children to work independently fosters the 'can-do' attitude. Children who have the 'can-do' attitude see failure as part of life and learning. To foster a positive attitude towards challenge, show an interest when a child is facing difficulty but avoid solving his problems for him. Be matter-of-fact about failure, and analyse it without attaching emotion to it. Ask questions about it, and help the child to problem-solve. Maybe another child could help, or maybe the whole group could get involved. Maybe different materials need to be used, or maybe it would be better to try again tomorrow when everyone has had a chance to think about possible solutions. Maybe success is going to take several days, or several weeks, and interim targets need to be made to give structure to the process and a sense of progress.

The language used with children will affect their attitudes towards challenge. A useful tool is to use the phrase 'not yet'. The 'Traffic Light' system has a red light, but the meaning is 'I don't understand *yet*' rather than 'I don't understand'. When a child finds that she cannot do something, the response should be, 'I know you cannot do it *yet*, but you will be able to soon. How can we help you to learn to do it?'

The 'Traffic Light' is described on page 96.

With a 'can-do' attitude, the child is eager to learn, and he is able to learn *about* learning. He has a good selection of tools and no holes in his self-esteem pockets. He is emotionally literate. He is ready to learn.

Step 5: Managing behaviour positively

Tools for managing behaviour

> *One test of the correctness of educational procedure is the happiness of the child.*

Maria Montessori

> I am good at tidying up and so is Frances.

Jon, aged three

Our aim in the early years is to help children to understand what constitutes appropriate behaviour and to help them to self-manage their behaviour. This self-control is a part of what constitutes emotional intelligence. We need to decide what our expectations are, making them appropriate to children's age and developmental stage. Many practitioners draw up a simple set of rules for their setting. In order to be effective, it is essential that any set of rules is drawn up with the children and not simply imposed upon them. This process helps them to understand the reasons behind the rules and makes it more likely that they will follow them.

Rules should be phrased positively. 'Put away the toys when you have finished playing with them,' is a lot more positive than, 'Don't leave toys on the floor.'

Matching activities to the needs of the children against a background of a clear and agreed code of conduct will decrease the likelihood of undesirable behaviour. Doing this will foster the children's intrinsic motivation to learn, which in turn leads to them being motivated to behave appropriately. When the curriculum is appropriate and the right level of stimulation and challenge is offered, the other strategies that we have discussed in the last few chapters will become increasingly powerful. When children's physical needs are met and they have emotional intelligence, high self-esteem and a 'can-do' attitude, they will exhibit good learning behaviours.

But, of course, every practitioner knows that there are children who exhibit challenging and inappropriate behaviour due to factors that are outside the practitioner's control. For these children, the provision of an exciting and appropriate curriculum may not be enough, and a more direct behavioural approach needs to be taken. In these cases, a behaviour programme sometimes becomes necessary. This means that the process by which targets are going to be achieved is formally discussed and recorded, and the plan immediately becomes more likely to succeed.

The key to a successful behaviour programme is to devise good targets, which are then linked to an action plan. Good targets are SMART:

 S pecific: if a target is vague, it will not be successful. Be as specific as you can: when and where do you want this behaviour to occur? How often? With whom? In what sized group? At what times of day?

 M easurable: in order to assess whether a target is measurable, ask the question, 'How will we know that the target has been achieved?'

 A chievable: too many targets will be too difficult to implement at one time. Tackle the most important aspects of behaviour first, and move onto others later.

 R ealistic: targets need to be related to small steps, rather than lofty aims that cannot easily or quickly be achieved.

 T ime bonded: set a time within which you expect the target to have been reached. This should not be too long; with young children six or eight weeks should be a maximum.

These targets are only of value if they are shared with parents or carers and all those who work with the child, and then linked to a clear action plan. Some practitioners choose to also share the target directly with the child. For each target, details need to be given about how the target will be achieved. For example, last year, when Kishan attended a day care centre, the practitioners wanted him to be able to sit on the mat for story times without shouting out inappropriately or disturbing other children by touching or climbing across them. They drew up the target: *To be able to sit on the mat for one short story (maximum four minutes) without touching other children.*

The practitioners made the decision at this stage to focus on helping Kishan to learn to sit still and not to try to modify his inappropriate shouting out. After Kishan had achieved this target, they agreed that they would draw up a further action plan to help him to learn not to call out. They included a specific time limit to the length of time that they would expect Kishan to sit so that there was no ambiguity about their aims.

The next stage was to decide how they would help Kishan to achieve this target. Their action plan included ideas about how they would use *The Three As* system, which we discuss in the next section, to help them to achieve the goal:

Mrs X to sit on chair by door during story time. Kishan to sit by her feet. Mrs X to use affirmation, 'Kishan is good at sitting still' before the story begins.

If Kishan tries to move away, Mrs X to put hands on his shoulders and turn him gently back.

If Kishan continues to move away, Mrs X to calmly take him to the Quiet Area to read a book of his choice, then allow him to play for the remainder of story time.

If Kishan sits for the short story, Mrs X to acknowledge by giving non-verbal feedback and then taking him to the Quiet Area to play until story time is over.

By being very specific about how a target is going to be achieved, the chances of success are raised considerably. Notice that the practitioners did not include any direct reward system in their action plan. They planned to use affirmations and acknowledgement, but decided that Kishan's target and behaviour was not challenging enough to warrant an extrinsic motivator such as a sticker chart. They wanted him to learn to modify his behaviour for its own sake. The 'reward' for Kishan of learning to sit for the story time was to be the pleasure of hearing the story itself: Kishan needed to become self-motivated to sit and listen.

Yet other children, usually due to external factors that are outside the practitioner's control, do need a method using extrinsic motivators to modify their behaviour. In these cases, the important principle is that the reward system must be used only for as long as it takes to modify the behaviour, and no longer. The child needs to learn that the appropriate behaviour brings about its own rewards, and so the practitioner needs to work hard to help the child to 'wean' from extrinsic rewards.

Mikey entered reception class half way through the spring term. He had attended three schools previously and was now in his fourth foster home. Understandably, Mikey had little trust that the adults around him would remain consistent. He intended, it seemed, to prove that he was 'unlovable'. He refused to follow directions, often choosing to do the exact opposite of what was asked. If the children were sitting on the mat, Mikey would go to sit on a chair at the other end of the room. If they were lining up, he would hide under a desk or run to the door, pushing children out of his way as he went. He rarely settled to a task for more than a few seconds.

With the help of the educational psychologist, Mikey's teacher drew up a behaviour plan for him that targeted his most disruptive behaviours first – the ones that she thought would have the most positive impact on Mikey and the class if they were modified. It was vital that Mikey would feel immediate success so that his self-esteem could receive a much-needed boost. Mikey clearly needed an extrinsic reward system to help him break out of the habit of this disruptive behaviour.

But instead of simply making a sticker chart for Mikey 'behaving well' or 'being good', the teacher broke down her aims into small, manageable targets that Mikey would be successful in achieving. She linked the targets to a clear action plan showing how each was to be achieved. For example, Mikey was given a chair beside the mat to sit on when he didn't want to sit with the other children. The teacher put his name on it, and explained to the class that Mikey was to have the chair while he was settling in. At story times, Mikey was asked if he would rather sit on the mat, or on the chair. He received a sticker or a smiley face for sitting on either. Giving children a choice in this way usually removes the temptation for the child to refuse to comply with your wishes, as he is being given the opportunity to make a decision for himself.

Each of Mikey's targets was planned in this way to guarantee that he had the support available to ensure success. By the end of each day, Mikey's sticker chart would be quite full. He could then choose to take it home or display it in class, or to put it in his drawer. When a reward system such as this is needed for a young child, the child needs to be able to see tangible progress being made. It is no good having to wait until after lunch or the end of the day for a sticker: the feedback needs to be frequent and immediate. Gradually, as the child is successful and his targets are being met, new targets and an action plan can be drawn up, until the child has reached a level of self-motivation.

A simple system for giving meaningful and positive feedback that will impact learning and behaviour is one called 'The Three As'. That is where we head to next: *The Three As – Acknowledgement, Approval and Affirmation.*

Brain-based learning for the early years foundation stage

Acknowledgement

Acknowledgement needs to be given in order for us to know that we are on the right track. This is equally as true for children as it is for adults. Acknowledgement also adds to the 'feel good factor' – and it makes the world go round!

If a colleague only reported on the negative aspects of your work, ignoring your positive achievements, how would you feel? What about if the feedback was positive, in spite of the fact that you knew there were some weaknesses in your work that day? Neither of these scenarios would optimize your learning. Acknowledgement of what you have achieved should help you to become more self-aware and self-critical. This is what we should be aiming for when we give feedback to the children in our care.

We should acknowledge achievements across the whole range of skills and children's development, not purely the academic achievements. Acknowledgement can be a powerful tool for encouraging appropriate social skills and behaviour. Yet it is easy to focus on the children who demand our attention. Numerous studies show that boys often demand more attention from teachers in classrooms across the school age range, both through assertive 'good' behaviour, and through challenging behaviour. For example, a study for the Scottish Council for Research in Education found that:

> ❛ *Contributions from boys predominate both physically and verbally during classroom interaction.*[44] ❜

Acknowledgement needs to be given to all children. It needs to be specific and direct, and should be given continually and consistently. It can be given verbally or non-verbally. The practitioner can smile, she can give a hug or a 'thumbs up' sign, she can give a pat on the back, or a round of applause, or any number of other gestures. For younger toddlers, verbal feedback needs to be very simple and clear, such as 'Thanks! You found your boots!' or 'That's it, two pieces of apple for you and two for me.' Along with the acknowledgement must come a clear explanation of what exactly is being acknowledged.

For example, three-year-old Martin walked to the park with his childminder several times each week. Every time they passed the fruit shop on the way, Martin would reach out and touch the fruit display. He seemed to find it impossible to resist! One day, before setting out, the childminder asked him, 'How could you stop yourself touching the fruit?' 'Put my hands in my pockets', said Martin. As they reached the shop, she looked down at him. He whispered, 'Put hands in pockets'. He managed to walk past without touching anything. The childminder gave Martin a hug. 'Well done,' she said. 'You remembered about your hands all by yourself. Let's tell your mum this evening.'

It is important to acknowledge success continuously, until it becomes an integral part of the children's lives. They can share in the acknowledgement of one another's successes, for example with a round of applause or a celebration song or a rhyme with actions. Eventually children will learn to spontaneously acknowledge achievements within the group, and can develop fun ways to give feedback. In one pre-school, the children sang this song when Thomas used the scissors successfully, to the tune of 'Old MacDonald had a Farm':

Oh, (Thomas) did it again

Eeee-i-eeee-i-oh

He's so smart he did it right

Eeee-i-eeee-i-oh

With a (snip snip) here

And a (snip snip) there

Here a (snip)

There a (snip)

Everywhere a (snip snip)

Oh (Thomas) did it again

Eeee-i-eeee-i-oh

This song was used for any achievements in the group, substituting the name and an appropriate description. Each time that a child's achievement is acknowledged, it adds to his or her level of self-esteem. It is like adding another tool into the child's self-esteem pockets. With pockets full of useful tools, learning is so much more fun!

Approval

when Mrs Wade is pleased with me she smiles and smiles. It makes her look very pretty and it makes me feel happy inside.

Pete, aged five

Once an achievement or behaviour has been acknowledged, the next stage is to show your approval. The purpose of showing approval is to give reassurance and encouragement, which will help to ensure that the behaviour is sustained and repeated. For some children, particularly those lacking in confidence, the need for you to show your approval is greater than for others. Some children may not need you to use this 'A' at all – they are motivated and confident enough to be able to respond to feedback without much 'stroking'. The extent to which you use each aspect or the whole of *The Three As* will vary from child to child, and from situation to situation. Your aim should be to eventually not have to give excessive signs of approval as all the children in your care become equally confident and self-motivated.

The timing of offering feedback can be critical. If you give it too soon, the child may be distracted and not retain her focus on the task; if you give it too late, she may have become unsure or discouraged. A clear statement works best: 'Gillian, I am pleased to see you sharing the counters with Henry' or 'I like the way that you are trying hard to do your buckle up, Donald.' Statements of approval are effective when they are direct, relevant and personal, rather than non-specific words such as, 'Good work, Gillian and Henry' or 'Good try, Donald.'

If non-specific words of praise are simply offered as a reaction to the child's efforts, a chain of events is likely to be started. First, the child will feel good, for a few minutes. He might sustain his current activity or behaviour, or even be inspired to try harder. Alternatively, he might not be able to identify what exactly was pleasing to you, and so his efforts will either cease or will go off track. Either way, he will probably soon need a further assurance from you – another stroke – to reassure or encourage him. He is now in danger of becoming hooked on praise. An analogy would be the difference between offering a nourishing snack or a sugary sweet. The sweet may please for a moment, but it will not really satisfy. The child is likely to crave more. The nourishing snack, by contrast, will have a long-term positive effect on the child's growth and development.

In his book *Punished by Rewards,* Alfie Kohn argues that the excessive use of praise has a detrimental effect on self-motivation:

> *Praise is no more effective at building a healthy self-concept. We do not become confident about our abilities (or convinced that we are basically good people) just because someone else says nice things to us.*[45]

Kohn argues that if praise is to be used, the practitioner should follow four basic rules:

 Don't praise people, only what people do.

 Make praise as specific as possible.

 Avoid phony praise.

 Avoid praise that sets up a competition.

Once the child knows that he has your approval, and what it is for, you can now move onto the last of *The Three As,* when you affirm that the success is going to be repeated.

Affirmation

Affirmations can be used to create the environment for success. Frequent affirmations of a child's best qualities and achievements will confirm in her mind that a success was not incidental and that it will be repeated. This is particularly important for children who have low self-esteem.

Affirmations to individuals tend to be more specific to the targets and aims for that child. For example, at the start of the year George's key person felt that George needed to become more assertive in group situations. Whenever she noticed that he was taking a passive role, she would make the affirmation, 'George is good at explaining his ideas', and if necessary follow up with, 'George, would you like to tell us what you think?'

Affirmations can also be used as a tool for instilling positive attitudes amongst groups. For example, the practitioners in one pre-school used the affirmation, 'We are all good at standing still when given the signal', when they gave a clap then raised their hands in the air to gain the attention of the children. For several weeks, some of the children found it difficult to remember what the signal meant, and would continue playing. But, after a while, these continual affirmations paid off and all the children became good at stopping at the signal. As each child learns to believe each positive affirmation, she is being provided with a useful self-belief to put in her self-esteem pockets.

Some practitioners design and display affirmation posters. Pictures, photographs, cartoons and captions can be used. The posters should directly refer to the types of behaviours and attitudes that you wish to foster. Other practitioners put affirmations to music. Music is a wonderful vehicle for influencing mood and for triggering memories. Using music utilizes the natural ability of the brain to make associations and recall things more easily. One practitioner used a glockenspiel to play a simple tune as she made affirmations, such as, 'We all sit beautifully on the mat.' Affirmations can be prefaced with the word 'you' if the practitioner is addressing the children, or by 'we' if the children are joining in.

The Three As system gives a simple structure to help set expectations and guide the behaviour of young children. It ensures that there is a consistent and positive approach within the setting and it presupposes that all children are capable of behaving appropriately. This positive attitude is one of the most powerful tools available to practitioners, and is an essential part of brain-based learning techniques. But, of course, parents have the greatest influence upon their child's attitudes and behaviour, and a partnership with them is essential if children are going to reach their potential. That is our next step: to consider how we can build that positive partnership approach with parents and carers.

Step 6: Fostering partnerships with parents and carers

> *We have clear evidence as children move through their early years, of the positive impact of parental engagement on children's cognitive and social development; as well as on numeracy and literacy skills.*

Every Parent Matters, DfES, 2007

> Mummy likes to come to nursery to play with me and the other children. She is good at painting and putting away the bricks.

Clara, aged four

Working in partnership with parents and carers

The parent or carer will have more influence on what the child learns, how she learns, and what she believes, than any practitioner, no matter what setting she attends. Therefore, the stronger the partnership between parents, carers and practitioners becomes, the more effective the education will be for the child. The political climate in recent years has become one where legislation is seen as a viable way to enforce home–school partnerships. There is an increasing legislative push to ensure that parents are empowered to influence policies that affect their children, with the Children's Plan of 2007 laying out clear expectations:

> *Parents bring up children, not governments, and we want this Children's Plan to mark the beginning of a new kind of relationship in which the Government commits to working in close partnership with families at every level, from making policy to delivering services.*

The move to legislate for parent involvement underscores most current education initiatives. Yet common sense would suggest that any legislation is not going to be as effective as the grass-roots hard work of creating links and building positive relationships. Attention to simple details about the setting is essential. Often those who work in a setting can lose sight of the impression that might be given to a newcomer, and so it is important to stand back and assess the setting objectively every once in a while.

One school had a policy of recruiting a volunteer who had never been to the nursery to arrange to visit for a session. After this, the volunteer would give feedback to the staff about the experience. These volunteers would be asked to mention even seemingly minor details, such as how easy they found it to park and find the main entrance. The staff would then brainstorm ideas about how to improve their systems for welcoming visitors and giving the appropriate information and impression. An alternative way to do this is to elect a member of staff, a colleague or a friend to do this and act as an impartial observer for an hour or two. You might wish to draw up a list of questions to ask the volunteer.

Once you are sure that your setting is warm and welcoming to newcomers, you need to consider the effectiveness of your lines of communication with parents and carers. In the most successful settings there are strong formal and informal systems for communication. The informal aspect of parent–practitioner communication starts at the front door. An available, welcoming, smiling practitioner will automatically build good relationships. But a frequent challenge facing many practitioners is that there are some parents or carers who demand more of the practitioner's time at the beginning or end of the day than is practical. There is a difference between a parent quickly mentioning that her child has a sore toe and so must not take off her shoes in the sandpit, and a parent who wants to engage in a lengthy discussion about her child's language development first thing in the morning! By giving plenty of opportunities for lengthier discussions, the need for parents to engage staff during the working day is diminished. A regular schedule of parent conferences ensures that these issues can be dealt with outside of the normal working week. Wise practitioners keep their diary to hand at the start and end of each day. This way they can easily say, 'That sounds important. Why don't we make a time when we can talk comfortably?'

In addition to giving feedback at formal meetings and parent conferences, it is important to give parents regular informal updates about children's progress. These informal 'chats' serve two purposes: they give the parent important information about her child, and they help to build trust between the two adults. The key to good partnerships is that the parent really knows that the practitioner understands and cares about the child.

Another useful way to build good partnerships is to have a clear 'induction' programme for new children and families. It is worth investing time in organizing a few afternoons for children to visit, with maybe some special activities, and a gradual build-up to a time when the parents can move away for a discussion while their children play. As part of their induction schedule, some practitioners include home visits. One nursery school made a home visit to every new child before he or she started school. The children were really excited to be able to show off their house, pets, bedroom and toys. The only complaint that the staff had about the system was that they were so well entertained in the children's homes that they would gain weight from all the cakes and goodies that they were offered!

The most successful settings also have good systems for ensuring that there is clear communication about everyday events and activities. In some communities the parents welcome regular, lengthy newsletters that explain everything in detail. In other communities, it is more appropriate to give brief 'flyers', blog spots, web links or weekly emails, while having informal talks about important announcements or forthcoming events. Coffee mornings or after-school meetings can ensure that information is made available to parents. Some practitioners use a whiteboard or large notice board to give information. It is important to be mindful of the fact that different families have differing challenges due to work and childcare schedules. Sometimes regular telephone calls or emails help to maintain lines of communication, particularly with working parents. Some settings and schools share achievements by posting photos of current activities in a pictorial diary on their website, with pages for each group or class.

In many communities, parents also appreciate the opportunity to learn more about child development and relevant parenting issues, for example from visiting speakers such as speech therapists, paediatric nurses, health visitors, or midwives. Some settings get together to organize meetings where they screen DVDs about important parenting topics, followed by a discussion. Some practitioners lend parents leaflets and books about child development, health issues and practical ideas for play activities. The Bookstart programme should provide every family with packs of age-appropriate books and materials for their children, along with invitations to join the local library, and some practitioners choose to work with parents to expand on this programme.[46] One nursery school suggested to parents that instead of giving practitioners end-of-term gifts, they might prefer to make donations of simple paperback books to the class lending libraries, or contribute to suggested titles for their adults' library, where parents could browse or borrow books.

Researchers Ghazvini and Readdick analysed the frequency of communication with parents in a variety of settings alongside the quality of education offered.[47] In the settings that were of higher general quality, the parents and caregivers reported higher levels of communication with the staff. The quality of the partnerships and communication between the home and the setting will depend also upon the ways that parents are involved in the everyday life of the setting. Different individuals have different things to offer the early years setting, but we should work from the fundamental belief that *everybody has something to offer*. Some parents prefer to play a low-profile role, whereas others have the time and desire to be involved in more ambitious projects.

One nursery teacher, realizing that she had a group of parents who did not seem comfortable working within the setting, asked for volunteers to help her to organize a resource box for her displays. It was difficult for her to find the time to cut out enough letters for titles on displays or to make interesting and imaginative borders for the boards. The parents took over the organization of the display resources. They met together for coffee twice a month and eventually started organizing complete displays. In this way, a group of parents who were initially not comfortable working within the setting found a way to contribute with confidence.

A child who knows that his parents and practitioners are working together as a team can be relaxed, confident and emotionally secure in the learning environment. When his emotional needs are taken care of in this way, he is more likely to develop the 'can-do' attitude and have strong self-esteem. With this secure foundation, he is able to focus on playing and learning and is able to reach his full potential.

Extended provision in schools and settings

Over the past decade there has been a significant shift in the expectations of the role of schools. No longer does a school act independently in traditional school hours, and no longer do childcare providers work in isolation. Children's Centres, Extended Schools and Neighbourhood Nurseries are becoming shared communities where coordinated early years services are available on one site. Clearly, the current political agenda is to try to coordinate services and so raise the quality of life of individual families. Indeed, it is an aim that children's centres will *'lift children out of poverty by enabling parents to work and to improve both educational and healthy outcomes for children'.*[48]

There are obvious advantages in coordinating different agencies and individuals to work together. In many children's centres, childminders attend 'stay and play' sessions with their minded children, so creating an opportunity for practitioners to learn as the children benefit from the social experience. Others share skills through staff training or parent education sessions. Parents who in the past had little access to any form of parenting education can now find resources on many aspects of parenting on one site. The benefits are self-evident.

This extension of children's services is viewed as essential to the success of *Every Child Matters*:

' *Extended schools are a key delivery mechanism for the five outcomes which children and young people themselves have identified as being important to them: being healthy, staying safe, enjoying and achieving, making a positive contribution and achieving economic wellbeing.*[49] '

All families are now to have equal access to children's services, including high-quality childcare for those aged between three and fourteen from 8 a.m. to 6 p.m., five days per week, 48 weeks per year. Free early years provision for three and four-year-olds is rising to 20 hours per week, 38 weeks per year. The most disadvantaged two-year-olds across the UK are now receiving free part-time early learning and childcare provision, with the aim of ultimately providing this service to all two-year-olds.

With this change in society's expectations and provision for young children, it would be easy to focus our attention on providing care, coordinating resources, educating parents and providers, and improving facilities, without relating what we do to what research has shown about child development. We know that the most vital period for laying foundations for healthy emotional development is the first three or four years. These are the years within which we are now embarking on one of the largest social experiments of all time, and we are continuing to experiment as children enter school.

Between birth and the age of six months, babies do not demonstrate stranger anxiety, and are usually happy to be comforted by any warm, reassuring adult. That is not to say that they do not recognize their mothers, but until the age of approximately six months, there will be little anxiety if the baby is handed to another adult. The reason for this is probably two-fold. First, the baby is not mobile and has not developed that sense of urgency about separation. Second, until the age of about six months, the brain's frontal lobes have not developed well enough to grasp what Jean Piaget called 'object permanence'. Quite literally, the baby does not yet have the cognitive ability to feel anxiety about his mother leaving him. But, as all new mothers find out, once that wiring is in place, a previously content and relaxed baby can become highly agitated whenever she leaves the room, and can create an embarrassing scene if a well-meaning stranger talks to him in the supermarket!

The original researcher on attachment theory was John Bowlby from London's Tavistock Clinic. Bowlby's theory that a strong mother–child bond was essential to mental wellbeing resulted in more humane practices when children were hospitalized. In his report to the World Health Organization in 1951, Bowlby espoused the importance of working with families in order to protect children and raise them from deprivation:

> *Just as children are absolutely dependent on their parents for sustenance, so in all but the most primitive communities, are parents, especially their mothers, dependent on a greater society for economic provision. If a community values its children it must cherish their parents.*[50]

Subsequent work by Mary Ainsworth in the 1960s attempted to categorize the levels of attachment shown by children in what was called *A Strange Situation*. Children were observed as they played in a room while their parent traded places with a stranger. Ainsworth was interested in how the children would respond to the departure and return of their caregiver. This led to her theory that attachment can fall into different categories, depending on the level of security in the adult–child bond. There have been many other subsequent studies on attachment but, ironically, Bowlby's and Ainsworth's work are used to both support and condemn the use of childcare, depending on the author's viewpoint.

No matter how we interpret the research, there is no doubt that secure attachment to the main caregiver and to other significant adults is the cornerstone for healthy emotional growth. Without it, we have a child and, ultimately, an adult who is unable to function successfully in society. Yet in recent years there has been a tendency to dismiss any research on attachment that does not fit with ideology, as experts and laypeople get involved in the never-ending 'mummy wars'. Opinions about working mothers should be set aside as we consider the evidence. Politicians need to forget political and economic agendas and seriously consider the research on attachment when creating policies that affect young children. Professionals need to put time and energy into supporting strong child–parent attachments, and carers need to work hard to meet children's attachment needs.

The most effective way to provide for secure attachment within the setting is the 'key person' approach. Identifying a named key person for every child is now a legal requirement for all children in out-of-home care from birth to the end of reception class. The key person role carries with it a deep commitment to the emotional needs of the child. This is more than being the worker who changes the nappies, serves the snack and reads the story. Authors Elinor Goldschmeid, Peter Elfer and Dorothy Selleck point out in their book *Key Persons in the Nursery – Building Relationships for Quality Provision* that the key person structure '*needs to be motivated and driven by a spirit of advocacy for the rights of children to be listened to, even before they can speak*'.[51] The key person purposely makes connections with the parent or carer each morning and evening. She ensures that the child knows that she is 'kept in mind' by the parent, and facilitates relationships between the child and others. She develops a genuine, secure bond with the child, and so forms one corner of 'a triangle of relationships' between the parent, the child and herself.

In November 2004, the government-sponsored Effective Provision of Pre-School Education (EPPE) project reported that children benefit from early years education, and that, '*pre-school can help to ameliorate the effects of social disadvantage and can provide children with a better start to school*'.[52] The value of high-quality provision was found to have a lasting effect through Key Stage 1, especially for children from disadvantaged backgrounds. The results suggested that pre-schools might be an effective intervention in reducing special needs, especially in the most disadvantaged children. Starting before the age of three gave some advantage in intellectual attainment, although the researchers found that it also contributed to some *'increased behaviour problems for a small group of children when they were 3 and again at 5'*. There was *'no evidence that full-day attendance led to better development than half-day attendance'*. The results of this study seemed therefore to support the current level of investment in part-time early years provision for over-threes.

EPPSE, the follow-up study to EPPE, which follows the children through to age 16, has found that the advantages of providing high-quality pre-school to disadvantaged families can be sustained if supported by a high standard of parenting. In a study for the Equalities Review, researcher Iram Siraj-Blatchford interviewed some of the families whose children were successful in spite of social and economic challenges, and found that in each of these families there was *'strong evidence of an adult or adults in the children's life taking parenting seriously and valuing education'*.[53] This evidence seems to point to the wisdom of making increased investment in parent support and education alongside continuing to provide and monitor quality pre-school education.

While it is generally accepted that the level of provision for over-threes in Britain is appropriate, there has been an increasing voice of concern amongst experts about where the government could be heading, with younger and younger children spending increasing amounts of time in childcare and older children spending longer hours in school. The government has itself acknowledged that it can sometimes seem that they do not value parents who stay at home:

> *In our research with parents, they told us that when we promoted the value of childcare for child development we sometimes seemed to downgrade the value of what they were doing as parents.*[54]

On the acknowledgements page of his book *Raising Babies – Why Your Love Is Best*, respected author Steve Biddulph opens with the statement that, *'This book took a long time to write, and a lot of courage to publish.'*[55] Biddulph acknowledges the great value of early childhood education for older children, but has great concern about the emotional and social development of children who spend long hours in care before the age of three:

> *This book presents much objective evidence, but it also carries a strong professional opinion for which I don't apologize. It is likely that some people will feel angry after reading it, and it may be unsettling for those who feel trapped by economic circumstances into placing their babies and toddlers in day nurseries when they would rather not. But my responsibility as a psychologist and educator is to be honest and to convey current findings and knowledge without gloss or deception.*

Education consultant and writer Sue Palmer expresses similar concerns in her book *Toxic Childhood – How the Modern World is Damaging our Children and What We Can Do About It*. In a country where children begin formal education at a very much younger age than those in the rest of Europe yet do not achieve more academically in the long run, Palmer feels that the government is investing in a dangerous experiment. She points out that while extended schools are vital for some families, we need to ask the question, '*how do children feel about being penned up in the same institution for up to ten hours a day, five days a week, forty-eight weeks a year?*'

In a ground-breaking book about the overworked and often exploited British worker, *Willing Slaves – How the Overwork Culture is Ruling our Lives,* journalist Madeleine Bunting examines how policy is fuelled by the notion that government funding must drive parents back to the workplace. Bunting believes that we are creating a '*Generation of the Anxious*' and particularly warns against any move towards extending full-time childcare below the age of three.

Of course, the reality is that there are families who need wrap-around care, and there are many children who benefit from it. Indeed, some children thrive on schedules where they move from carer to school to carer and then home. Others enjoy the benefits of staying in one setting with the same adults for the entire day. Many parents successfully combine care within extended family with flexible provision at a children's centre or school. Some parents would be miserable at home but are fulfilled when able to work, while others would welcome the opportunity to be free of financial ties to the workplace. No two children or families are the same, and there are no absolutes.

The only fair answer to the question of who should look after the children should be that there should be options and choice. Offering incentives for taking up more childcare in a society where families struggle and women often end up working unreasonable hours in poor conditions for low pay, is not offering choice. It is offering a survival strategy. At a time when more parents are becoming financially vulnerable, it would seem wise to offer the choice of aid to stay at home alongside current childcare incentives. The economic arguments for getting all mothers back to work make little sense, as subsidizing high quality childcare for the youngest children has been shown to cost as much as aiding those parents to stay home.[56] Times might have changed, but the fundamental needs of children and families have not. Investing in helping all parents make a *genuine choice* would be a wise investment in the future emotional health of children, their families, and so in the future of the country.

Plenary

Here are some points for reflection:

How are the physical needs of children met in your setting? What obstacles might lie in your way as you try to provide for these needs? How might you overcome these obstacles?

How do you describe the challenges of inclusion in your setting? How do you support parents of children with special needs, and how do you support colleagues and build relationships with outside agencies? How do your resources reflect an inclusive society?

Are the children in your care emotionally literate? Which children seem the most emotionally literate? Which of them seem to need help to manage their emotions? How might you address emotional literacy in your setting?

Which children in your care have a good set of tools for learning? How do you provide for the development of these positive attitudes? How do you work to support children's self-esteem and promote a 'can-do' attitude? Could you make more use of circle time to actively promote strong self-esteem?

How positive is the behaviour management in your setting? How do you work to help children to learn to manage their behaviour? How might *The Three As* system help you to reinforce good behaviour, manage challenging behaviour, and foster high self-esteem?

How would you describe the partnerships that you have in your setting with parents and carers? How well do you support children's attachment through the key person approach? How do you liaise with other providers of extended care? Are there any parents or carers who are not involved in any active partnership with staff? Are there parents who are struggling with the demands of balancing work and home? How might you address the needs of these parents and their children?

Where do we go from here?

Once children's physiological and emotional needs are catered for, they are ready to learn. If their behaviour is managed positively and there are strong links between home and the setting, their learning will be all the more effective.

Now we will move on to consider how to support independent learning through careful management of the environment, helping children to develop good listening and concentration skills, and ensuring that the feedback given is positive and supportive.

Supporting independent learning

The Big Picture

In this section you will:

Step 1: Consider how to organize your space in order to implement brain-based learning techniques, and read about ways that other practitioners have maximized the use of their environments

Step 2: Read about how children learn to pay attention and discover some ways to help them to improve their attention skills

Step 3: Consider what is appropriate when expecting children to stay on task and read about some ways to help them to increase their concentration span

Step 4: Think about the type of language used in the setting by both adults and children, and consider how to question and give good feedback

Step 1: Making maximum use of the environment

Organization of the learning environment

Within the acclaimed Reggio Emilia schools in Italy, careful attention is given to the look and feel of the classroom. Areas are organized for groups of various sizes to work on projects and displays are carefully formed at both adult and child eye-level. Common areas are designed to encourage interactions between children from different groups. Materials are arranged in ways that ensure that they are aesthetically pleasing and use is made of mirrors, plants and interesting artefacts to engage and inform the learner. In fact, the environment is considered so important that it is referred to as the *'third teacher'*.

> *The most effective kind of education is that the child should play amongst beautiful things.*

Plato

The practitioner needs to create a secure environment within which children can play and work. Children need space in which they can move, ideally moving freely between an outdoor area and the indoors. Materials need to be organized so that children can access them easily. Children need to be taught how to select and use materials appropriately and safely. Some practitioners play games where they set a hypothetical challenge, such as 'Go and fetch what you might need to make a model in the technology area.' The children can then go as individuals or groups to fetch whatever might be needed for this specific task. They can then return the materials to their correct places, as the practitioner talks through their actions, so adding language to the activity and rooting the experience more firmly in the children's memory.

We discuss the use of outdoor space for maximizing learning on page 114.

Practitioners who use brain-based learning techniques find that there are some additional materials that are indispensable in their work. Most of these are everyday items. Here is a list of some items that you might find useful in introducing the ideas in this book:

 A copy of the 'brain-based learning circle'

 A board at children's eye-level for displaying the To Do list

 A traffic light for checking understanding

 A whiteboard or pin-board for displaying the Big Picture

 A CD player with a number of music CDs or an MP3 player

 A large amount of blu-tac for sticking up posters, affirmations and mind maps

Sets of coloured pens or chalks for brainstorming sessions

 Pieces of card and paper of various colours and sizes for mind maps

 Sets of affirmation posters

 A 'Decibel Clock' for showing children your expectations for the noise level

 Props for circle time activities such as hats and soft toys

 Magic wands and different types of pointers for Brain Gym® exercises

 A list or 'menu' of brain-break ideas

 Lengths of ribbon and coloured pegs for displaying posters, pictures or mind maps

 Posters outlining rules and 'good sitting' and 'good listening'

 Traffic Lights, Good Listening posters and other brain-based learning resources can be found at www.alite.co.uk.

In some situations it is easier to maintain an ideal environment than in others. Many practitioners have the challenge of having to share their environment. Some practical solutions for overcoming this challenge include:

 Making laminated labels for each area of the room

 Using transparent boxes and bags for equipment

 Colour-coding boxes of equipment according to their contents

 Using boxes and trolleys with wheels

 Hanging display boards on hooks on the wall

 Using free-standing display boards

 Using boxes covered with fabric for 3D displays

 Using carpet samples to create comfortable book areas or home corners

For childminders the environment is naturally more one of a 'home' than a classroom, yet many of the principles of classroom organization still hold true. For example, providing a pin-board for a To Do list is as important in this type of setting as in the classroom. A cosy child's book area can be created in the corner of a room or even behind a sofa, and children can be taught to select materials independently from well-organized shelves of art materials or labelled boxes of toys.

A free-standing display board can be used during the day, but stored away when children go home.

Whatever your situation, it is worth taking time periodically to re-evaluate the use of space in your setting. Sometimes it helps to do this with a colleague or friend who can give new ideas. Another way to evaluate the learning environment is to list the desirable aspects of each area. Rather than being restricted by the limitations of your current situation, be idealistic when you do this, and imagine your perfect book corner, art area or home corner. List all the desirable items down one side of the paper, and make notes about how you might achieve this down the other side. Don't worry if you cannot meet all your ideals at once – you can build on the plan as finances become available or when new ideas or opportunities emerge.

Some practitioners like to spend time reorganizing their room with the children's help. Obviously, heavy furniture has to be handled by adults, but the children can help with ideas. One reception class teacher discussed possible changes to the layout of the room with her class by drawing diagrams on a whiteboard. Another practitioner told how she found a solution to help the three-year-olds in her pre-school group learn to put materials back in the correct place:

I was spending twenty minutes each evening sorting out pencils, crayons, glue spreaders, and so on into their correct containers and putting them on the right shelves. I went to visit our local infant school, where the reception teacher had a system for helping children to tidy properly. Each type of material was kept in a different-shaped container. On each container was a drawing so that children could see what should go in each pot. She had then covered the shelves with sugar paper. She had drawn around the outline of the pot and in the centre had drawn a simple picture of the item to match the pot. It was so simple!

I altered the system a little to help my youngest children, by colour coding the pots. There was an immediate improvement in the children's independence in tidying. At tidy-up time my only problem for a few days was that every child wanted to tidy the pots, and nobody wanted to tidy up elsewhere!

A well-organized environment invites desirable learning behaviours. Sometimes even a slight alteration to the organization of the environment can make a significant difference to learning and behaviour. For example, a newly qualified teacher described a difficulty that she had with the children running in the classroom:

One afternoon the Headteacher taught the class while I went on a course. The next day I was amazed to find that I didn't have to say 'Don't run' to a single child! The Headteacher had simply shifted a few of the tables a foot or so in one or other direction. There were no longer any clear 'runways' from one activity to another, and the children had to walk in order to negotiate their way around the furniture. Now, the moment I have to ask children to walk in the classroom, I stand back and look at the layout of the room to see how I can alter it to foster good behaviour.

Another practitioner enters her classroom on her knees once every few weeks, to see what the environment looks like to a young child. As a result of her first viewing of her setting from a child's level, she had all her display boards moved down by several feet. Other ways to assess the environment include asking a new or temporary practitioner to give you feedback about how easy she found it to work with your children, or seeing if a different group of children can tidy up successfully.

Display

 I do paintings for Angela to put on the kitchen wall. I use lots of red because it's my favourite colour. I think Angela likes it too.

Bonnie, aged four

Many practitioners find that when they begin to use brain-based learning techniques, they find themselves questioning long-held beliefs about displaying children's work. Your purpose for display will differ according to individual circumstances. However, in any setting display should:

 create a sense of belonging

 motivate towards further learning

 enhance learning

 aid recall

invite children to be interactive

 celebrate and affirm success

 stimulate further thinking

 remind of rules and behavioural codes

 help children to make connections between concepts

For many young children, their first painting on the wall marks an important moment – they now 'belong' in this community – their painting is there, with their name emblazoned upon it – to prove that they belong. It is usually a mistake to wait until Friday to display the work done during the week. A rapid system is needed to mount work and get it on the walls while the memory is still fresh in the children's minds. Time spent in advance on preparing display boards means that display can be more immediate and meaningful for the children.

In addition to featuring the children's work, displays should inform and challenge children to think. They need to be interactive and enhance learning. They need to be three-dimensional! Young children often need to touch in order to fully understand. Tactile experience is essential to their learning. A piece of brightly coloured fabric thrown over a table, or over a pile of sturdy cardboard boxes arranged at different heights, can be used to make these displays.

The Thinking Child

Brain-based learning for the early years foundation stage

The items for these three-dimensional displays need to be exciting – but this does not mean that they necessarily have to be exotic. Most artefacts can be used in many different contexts. For example, a lavender candle given to you by an elderly aunt last Christmas could be incorporated into a display about light, or one about festivals, or colours, or shape, or materials. A mention in a newsletter or an email to parents saying that next week you intend to make a display about insects or fish can yield some fascinating artefacts!

Captions and pictures on cards can be used to generate interest and deeper thinking. One practitioner would set challenges on caption cards, such as 'Can you find out how many legs a spider has?' The answer would be written under a flap. A parent would often work with individuals or pairs of children to read the captions and respond, and the captions would be updated regularly to increase the level of challenge. After a while, the children started to make their own caption cards. This involvement of children in the process of building displays gives them an increased sense of ownership. Including fiction and non-fiction books in displays helps to foster a sense of reading for purpose. Children soon learn to pick out relevant books and other items of interest and add them into the display. Stands that display the appropriate page of a book help children to work independently.

Find out more about 'good sitting' and 'good listening' on pages 84-8.

You also need to allow space to display affirmation posters. Ask children to help to make them and then put them up. Refer to them frequently. Likewise, posters about skills such as 'good sitting' and 'good listening', or about group rules or codes of behaviour help reinforce positive learning behaviours. Other posters can celebrate the successes of individuals and groups. Photographs can be powerful and personal reminders of success, in addition to fostering a sense of community and belonging. Digital photo-frames can be used to show pictures of events and children's achievements.

Many practitioners assign an area for children to display their own work. Here the children can be as creative as they wish. The paper, cutting and sticking materials for display can be made freely available. Depending on the age and maturity of the group, children can be taught how to use equipment, with adults then being available when they need to put their work up. The decision about how to display the work should be left to the children. They can be encouraged to write their own messages and captions for this board too. Even if George's caption reads to an adult as 'Toor er Goerg eeg rer', to George it clearly reads, 'This is George's red car'.

Display is more challenging for practitioners who work in shared settings. Many practitioners use one side of a free-standing board to display the previous week's work, and the other side for children's own work. Interactive 3D displays can be placed in front of free-standing boards or a wall, or can stand alone on covered boxes or tables. The key in these situations is good organization, such as laminating key caption cards and posters, clearly labelling storage boxes of artefacts, keeping books categorized and ordered, and using sturdy materials that withstand being repeatedly dismantled. Using plastic wallets and pockets, shoe tidies, wardrobe organizers and clothes airing racks can help to create imaginative interactive displays.

If you work in a larger setting, it is worth considering how you could use the entire environment for display. The cloakroom areas, the kitchen, the dining hall, the library and the corridors can all be used. One practitioner used ribbons hanging from the corridor ceiling to display the letters that she was teaching, or shapes, or coloured cards, or animals. She set challenges such as, 'See if you can spot any red triangles hanging from the ceiling today.'

Writing and regularly reviewing a display policy can help you to focus on how you support children's learning through display. You might wish to adapt the list of questions below to do this.

How do our displays:

 create a sense of belonging?

 enhance learning?

 motivate towards further learning?

 aid recall?

 invite children to be interactive?

 stimulate further thinking?

 help children to make connections between concepts?

 celebrate and affirm success?

 remind of rules and behavioural codes?

Once you have answered these questions, you can develop your policy and think of new ways to enhance learning through the displays in your setting.

Step 2: Helping children to develop good attention skills

> **"** *A good teacher, like a good entertainer, first must hold his audience's attention, then he can teach his lesson.* **"**

John Henrik Clarke author, teacher and historian[57]

> **"** I like listening to stories best of all. **"**

Aline, aged three

The development of listening skills

Good listening skills are one of the essential tools for our children as they grow and learn. Hearing is the sense that develops first in the womb, and before birth a baby has already developed tastes in what he likes to hear. Top of the list is usually the mother's voice. Newborns will turn towards their mother at birth, and many mothers report that their babies recognize familiar music that they listened to when pregnant.

Fascinating Fact

Tests where noises are played to a foetus show that most babies respond to sound by blinking at about 24 weeks, and that the auditory pathways of the central nervous system are mature by 28 weeks.

What was not known until recently, was that hearing makes an actual physical difference to the brain:

> **"** *In a child who is born deaf, the 50,000 nerve pathways that normally would carry sound messages from the ears to the brain are silent. The sound of the human voice, so essential for brain cells to learn language, can't get through and the cells wait in vain. Finally, as the infant grows older, brain cells can wait no longer and begin to look for other signals to process, such as those from visual stimuli.* **"**

Ronald Kotulak[58]

Kishan's mother was worried about his hearing when he was a toddler, although hearing tests showed that there was nothing wrong. Kishan was similar to many young children: when he became absorbed in play or physical activity he tuned out the sounds around him. Many parents worry that this failure to easily process verbal communication may be a symptom of

'Attention Deficit Disorder' (ADD) or 'Attention Deficit and Hyperactivity Disorder'(ADHD). The number of diagnoses of these disorders is sharply on the rise, not just in the UK, but also in most other developed nations. There are various opinions about the disorder, ranging from those who believe the symptoms to be the result of changes in parenting and society, to those who believe ADHD to be caused by mutations of specific genes.

The evidence is still too much in its infancy for us to draw firm conclusions either way. Scientists are researching to see if there are significant differences in the brains of children with an ADHD diagnosis. A study using brain imaging in 1996 by Castellanos et al.[59] showed that in ADHD children the areas of the brain that regulate attention are smaller, yet nobody knows what actually causes these differences. Castellanos hypothesized that the cause may be genetic, but others hypothesize that it is a question of cause and effect: that it is the lack of use of these areas of the brain that causes them to be underdeveloped. In other words, if children *do not practise how to pay attention*, they do not exercise that part of the brain that *enables them to pay attention*. It's rather like being unable to run because you are unfit. If you do not exercise, you will not get fit, and if you are really unfit, you will become unable to run, and so a vicious cycle develops.

The ongoing research into ADHD and consequent debate about the evidence is of particular significance to practitioners because these behaviour patterns usually surface between the ages of three and five. After all, many of the symptoms of ADHD could be argued to be simply the 'symptoms' of being four years old! Whatever the outcome of research projects, the number of children being diagnosed with this disorder is on the increase. The numbers of Ritalin prescriptions vary widely between different primary care trusts, with the highest in 2007 being Wirral, where over 14 per cent of children receive the drug.[60] The cost of Ritalin to the NHS is currently estimated to be over £1 million per month.[61] This is a sobering thought when you consider this statement from an article in *The Observer*, citing researcher Dr Nora Volkow:

> *Even in pill form, Ritalin blocked far more of the brain transporters that affect mood change and had a greater potency in the brain than cocaine.*[62]

A setting that demands that children sit for inappropriate tasks for inappropriate lengths of time will not help children to develop good concentration and impulse control, and to a large extent the appropriateness of the setting will either help or hinder children who might be diagnosed with ADHD. In every setting there are children who need help to learn to pay attention and to respond appropriately, because they find it difficult to respond to auditory cues. Kishan is a child who benefits from being given clear instructions and being forewarned that something is about to happen. His teacher often touches his shoulder before she speaks to him. She also prefaces each instruction with his name, giving him time to turn to look at her and prepare to listen. When Kishan is outside and involved in physical activity, she often needs to put her hands on his shoulders and stoop down to his level to speak to him. She frequently turns his head towards her when she speaks. Without this help to develop the skills of attention, Kishan would be at a disadvantage in his learning.

Processing time, when children can internalize concepts, is essential for meaningful learning, particularly for children such as Kishan. It needs to be built in during group and whole-class sessions in order for children to process and internalize new information. Children's attention levels tune in and out on natural cycles that are partly physiological and partly dictated by their level of interest in the activity. It is important to give time for all children to process information and avoid rushing through explanations or discussion times.

Many children have difficulty in paying sustained attention due to a hearing deficit. The National Deaf Children's Society estimates that some 80 per cent of children under eight years old experience periods of temporary deafness. Hearing difficulties account for a large proportion of children on special needs registers in schools, and many more cases remain undiagnosed. It is easy to mistake hearing loss for a behavioural difficulty or for general developmental delay. Half of deaf children remain undiagnosed by the age of 18 months and one quarter of deaf children are still not diagnosed by three years.[63] This means that a great deal of responsibility lies with the practitioner to be vigilant.

Children with hearing loss can be helped by careful management, with strategies such as making sure that you have the child's attention before speaking, positioning yourself in front of the child and getting down to her level, or ensuring that you can be seen by facing towards the light.

Teaching listening skills

Listening and sitting are skills that often need to be learned just as reading or writing. Some children enter early years education with well-developed listening skills, while others do not. To listen effectively requires that the child thinks, whereas hearing simply requires the child to be in the vicinity of the speaker! It is worth taking the time to teach these specific skills, and to reinforce this learning regularly. You can begin by referring to listening effectively as 'good listening' and sitting attentively as 'good sitting':

'Jamie, I can see that you are doing "good sitting". I like the way that you have your hands in your lap. Thank you!'

'Marcus is quiet and ready to do "good listening". He is looking at my face – well done!'

The principles of 'good sitting' and 'good listening' can be taught explicitly and displayed on posters on the wall. Children need to be reminded of the rules regularly. Here are some rules for 'good sitting' and 'good listening':

To do good sitting on the carpet you must:

 Put your bottom on the carpet

 Face the front

 Cross your legs

 Put your hands in your lap

To do good sitting on a chair you must:

 Put your bottom on the chair

 Face the front

 Keep all four legs on the floor

 Pull the chair in to the desk

To do good listening you must:

 Keep your hands still

 Look at the speaker

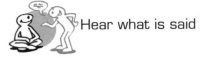

Hear what is said

Think about it

What is an acceptable noise level?

It is difficult to define what is an acceptable noise level in an early years setting. What is appropriate on one day or in one session or with one group of children might not be appropriate at another time. The measure of whether a noise level is appropriate has to come from observing what sort of activity is going on in the classroom and how successfully the children are learning. There are different noise levels that are appropriate for different areas of the classroom, and for indoor or outdoor play.

A more pertinent question, therefore, is probably, 'Is the noise level appropriate for the activities being undertaken, and does the language being used facilitate learning?' Do children in your care know what level of talk is appropriate for each type of activity? Do they understand that it is not appropriate to shout in a library, but that it is acceptable to shout during an action game outside? Can they listen to others in circle time and wait their turn before speaking? These are social skills that will ensure that the noise level in your setting is appropriate, no matter what activity is taking place.

It is important that children are taught about the appropriate types of voice to use in varying situations. Many children will learn this naturally, but others will need explicit teaching. A useful method for doing this is to use the 'Decibel Clock'. This is a clock face which is displayed prominently at the front of the room with different types of activities described on it with the level of noise for each type of activity: silence (0), pole-bridging (1), whispering (2), quiet talking (3) and talking (4). The practitioner turns the hand to the area of the clock face to show the noise level that she expects before the children begin the activity. Individual cards with cartoons showing the appropriate level can be given to groups or displayed in specific areas of the room such as the book corner or home corner.

Here are three more ways to teach children how to use an appropriate voice:

Use different voices when story-telling and encourage the children to practise them, such as muttering, whispering, quiet talking, calling to somebody, or shouting for help.

Use fingers to show the level of noise that you expect – a closed fist means silence, one means pole-bridging, two means whispering, and so on.

Use a chart with pictures of different-sized mouths, pointing to the size that represents the level of noise that is appropriate.

Gaining and maintaining children's attention

Inexperienced practitioners often find that one of the greatest challenges is gaining and holding children's attention. In the early years setting, this is particularly challenging. Children are encouraged to work and play independently, and materials are freely available. It is difficult for children then to learn that there are times when an adult requires them all to stop what they are doing and be quiet. Persuading ten or even 20 or 30 young children to do this at the same time is a daunting task!

The golden rule used by all successful practitioners is never to continue to speak when the children are not paying attention. To accept background noise and continue to speak is to give a clear signal that background noise is acceptable. Clarity about your expectations is vitally important. If you ask for quiet, you must settle for nothing less. For the time that you are addressing the children, it is quite reasonable to expect quiet, even from very young children, although obviously, the length of time that you expect them to maintain the quiet must be appropriate to their age and developmental stage.

It is a good idea to preface a request for quiet with a warning, to give children such as Kishan processing time. Just imagine watching a gripping movie at the cinema. Suddenly there is a power cut and the screen goes blank. You don't know what is happening. Will you ever see the rest of the movie? Will you ever find out what happened at the end? The emotions that you might feel in such a situation would be felt ten-fold by a child such as Kishan.

If a child such as Kishan is repeatedly forced to stop what he is doing without warning, one of two things is likely to happen. He may learn to conform to such rules, even though they ignore his developmental needs. Or he may find it impossible to conform, and act out his frustration in a number of ways: by having tantrums, by continuing his games quietly while seemingly cooperating with the practitioner, or by avoiding becoming focused on an activity because he half-expects it to be halted before it has begun. Luckily Kishan's teacher always gives ample warning that an activity is due to end. She also provides for children to return to

an absorbing activity at a later time. She has a table set aside especially for children to store models or pictures that represent unfinished business to busy five-year-olds.

An auditory cue such as a hand bell can be used to warn children that the session is soon to come to an end. Many practitioners tell children that they have ten minutes, then five, then two, then one, before asking them to stop work. One practitioner used a familiar piece of music towards the end of the day to signal that there was not much time left. This gave children a chance to wind down and finish what they were doing.

Here are four ways to obtain children's attention:

 Start by clapping your hands, gradually becoming quieter and quieter until you are tapping three, then two then one finger on your palm. Teach the children to copy until you silently put your hands in your lap and are ready to speak.

 Start by clicking your fingers in a rhythm, encouraging the children to copy. Move your hands in circles as you do so, growing slower and quieter until you cease and are ready to speak.

 Tap your chin with a finger, then make a circular motion, tapping your ears, head, mouth, nose and so on, while the children copy until you put your hands down and start to speak.

 Teach the children a variety of action rhymes for gaining attention, such as the one below:

Give me one, give me two,

Give me five, look at you,

Ready to listen, ready to see,

Ready to learn, now look at me.

Lining up strategies

I don't want a class full of obedient children. I want a class full of cooperative children.

Reception teacher

Moving from one activity to the next, coming in from the playground, or leading into assembly, lining up can present a major challenge to the inexperienced practitioner. There is often no necessity for forming a queue for moving from one place to another. In one school, children were encouraged to stand still when the bell rang, then on the second bell simply walk into the building. There was no pushing or running, and quiet conversation was allowed. If formal 'lining up' is required, it needs to be recognized that is a skill that often needs to be taught and practised. Any of the suggestions below can be used to help children to move in an orderly manner from one place to another:

 Line up to a familiar piece of music

 Line up while counting in ones or twos

 Line up while singing a favourite song

 Line up according to what children are wearing

 Line up while pretending to be cats, dogs, elephants or giraffes

 Line up using a song such as the one below:

This is the way we make a line,

Make a line, make a line,

This is the way we make a line,

On a cold and frosty morning.

(To the tune of 'Here We Go Round the Mulberry Bush')

One innovative reception teacher helped her class to get 'in the mood for food' in the lunch queue, with the train song below:

Coffee, coffee, coffee, coffee, (moving arms slowly like a train)
Cheese and biscuits, cheese and biscuits, cheese and biscuits,
cheese and biscuits, (gradually getting faster)
Beef and carrots, beef and carrots, beef and carrots,
beef and carrots, (faster)
Fish and chips, fish and chips, fish and chips, fish and chips,
(very fast)
S O U P (like a train whistle, pulling the cord to stop the train)

Now that we have considered the importance of helping children to develop good attention skills, we will move on to consider how to help them to stay on task.

Step 3: Helping children to stay on task

How much time should be 'on task'?

> *When a teacher complains that students are "off task" – a favorite bit of educational jargon – the behaviorist will leap to the rescue with a program to get them back "on" again. The more reasonable response to this complaint is to ask, "What's the task?"*

Alfie Kohn[64]

We so often hear the description of children being 'on task' or 'off task' that we can fail to think about its wider implications. The practitioner's aim should be to provide a curriculum that fully engages children and is responsive to each child's individual interests and learning needs. Her interventions should be timely so that each child spends his time engaged in purposeful activity, with the appropriate balance between child-initiated and adult-led activities. Her task is to support learning and intervene in an appropriate manner when she judges that concentration is waning. She might realize that a child needs some time to process her learning, and encourage her to move off to do something of her own choice, or she may choose to re-engage her or to adapt or expand the activity.

The overriding aim should be to help each individual child to develop improved concentration skills across a wide curriculum. However, sometimes a child will develop a strong interest in one type of activity and may be resistant to suggestions that he participate elsewhere. Sometimes the best response is to embrace the child's current interest and allow her to focus on that skill or area of interest until she naturally moves on. At other times, the child needs help to gain confidence and explore new activities. For example, when Samantha was three, she attended a pre-school, which was her first experience of a setting away from the home. At first, she was reluctant to settle to any activity. When no other children were playing in the home corner, she would go in there, but if another child entered, Samantha would begin wandering around the room again.

As time went on, Samantha began to play alongside other children for brief periods. She would come to sit with an adult and watch them work with the playdough or clay. Her ability to concentrate on a task in this setting was increasing. A few weeks later, Samantha started to participate in certain activities. By the end of the first term, her concentration span on activities in the pre-school setting was similar to her concentration span at home. The amount of time that she spent 'on task' during these weeks of adjustment was right for her.

So the answer to the question, 'How much time should be "on task"' is simple – it varies enormously, according to the individual child, and the task.

Structuring the less formal sessions
It is a mistake to think that enforcing formal sessions upon young children will hasten their development and accelerate their learning. In fact, what happens is quite the opposite. To provide a curriculum that is not appropriate to the age and developmental stage of the child is to inhibit his learning. Author Michael Gurian points out that self-directed learning is essential for optimal brain development:

For the developing brain, self direction has many advantages, especially that in a well led environment the mind gravitates towards learning what it needs to learn in order to grow. The brain has, to a great extent, its own blueprint of how to grow itself.[65]

Brain-based learning for the early years foundation stage

It is not realistic to try to set a mathematical ratio for what the balance between child-initiated and adult-led activity should be, and the EYFS guidance makes it clear that practitioners need to make this judgement themselves, within the context of their own school or setting.

By paying attention to each child's play, the practitioner can make interventions that help develop concentration skills. Carrie sometimes finds it difficult to settle at an activity for a sustained period. She often moves away before completing a task. Today Carrie is playing an imaginative game on the floor mat with the toy vehicles. She begins by lining up some of the buses at the bus station. Before she has made a line of more than four buses to be washed at the car wash, she has started to sort out the lorries into the car park. Before she has sorted more than six lorries, she has moved away to rummage in another box for some lions.

And so Carrie's game would continue, flitting from one idea to the next, if the teacher did not step in. The buses would not get washed, the lorries would never get parked, and the lions would not get captured, because the policeman would have had to leave to chase the elephants! Carrie's game is elaborate and imaginative, but she needs some help to follow a theme through. Her teacher sits down to talk about the buses. 'Oh, they are lined up to go through the car wash,' she says. 'What about the lorries? Are they muddy too? Where have they been today?'

'I know,' says Carrie, able to think clearly now that she has slowed down. 'The lorries could do this . . . '. The teacher helps her to use her imagination in a more constructive and rewarding way.

The timetable in Carrie's nursery classroom allows for plenty of opportunity for child-initiated play. The outdoor area is used throughout the day; there is no set playtime and children can choose freely whether to play inside or out. Short periods of time are set aside each day for structured group activities and music and story times. As the year progresses, children are gradually introduced to the more formal aspects of a school day. By being provided with an age-appropriate curriculum, the children develop at a natural and comfortable pace. It is a wise practitioner who realizes that development and learning go hand in hand and can be facilitated, but not forced.

Introducing the more formal sessions
These are potentially confusing times for practitioners. After years of following advice about the implementation of the literacy and numeracy strategies, the tide seems to be turning back towards a less prescriptive curriculum. Children need to be able to make connections between different aspects of learning, and a balance needs to be sought between 'subject' teaching and cross-curricular learning. The Williams Mathematics Review found that, while the content of numeracy sessions in school tends to be appropriate, children *'had too few opportunities to use and apply mathematics'*.[66] The EYFS makes it clear that children *'must be provided with opportunity and encouragement to use their skills in a range of situations and for a range of purposes'* and that they must experience a *'broad range of contexts in which they can explore, enjoy, learn, practise and talk about their developing understanding'*.[67]

Many educators feel reassured by the 2009 recommendations of the Independent Review of the Primary Curriculum, which stresses the importance of teaching literacy and numeracy skills while giving children plenty of practice in cross-curricular experiences, and are hopeful that the new primary curriculum framework will give practitioners greater flexibility to tailor the delivery of the curriculum to the needs of the children. It is heartening that while the final review, released at the end of 2009, stopped short of recommending that the age of compulsory school attendance being altered to six years old, it did call for debate upon the issue, and recommended that the foundation stage curriculum is extended in all schools to the age of seven at the end of Key Stage 1.[68]

Considering the wide range of types of early years settings and differences in school admission policies, the question that should be foremost in the minds of practitioners is this: 'How can I meet current requirements while taking into account the range of age and experience and maturity of the children in my setting?' For some children, even by the summer term, full structured sessions are too long, but for other children they are appropriate. It is vital that the delivery of any session is appropriate to the developmental needs of young children and takes into account their short attention span. Special consideration needs to be paid to individual needs such as the summer-born children, boys, children with English as an additional language, and those who need a less structured approach. The practitioner must work within the parameters of the children in her setting.

For those older children who are ready for the introduction of more sustained sessions, the simple structure described below can be used to help to fully engage young children with comparatively short attention spans.

The brain-based learning circle

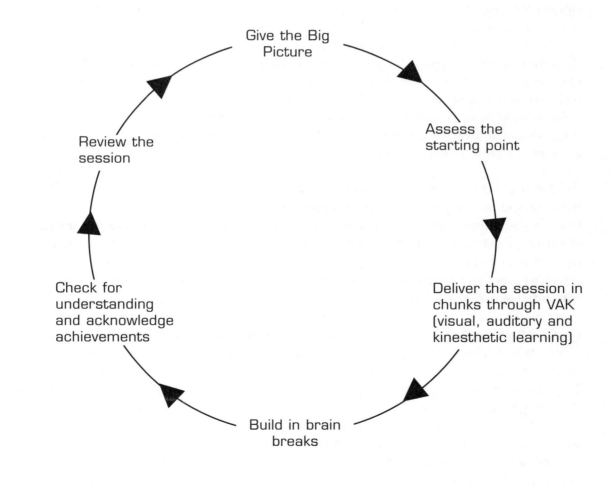

Give the Big Picture. This is an overview that is given at the start of the session. At this point it is important to ask open-ended questions and engage children's curiosity. It is also essential to allow time for the processing of information. Giving visual cues helps the visual learners. Clear repetition of key phrases helps the auditory learners. Using gestures or props helps the more kinesthetic learners. Give information in short 'sound bites' and when you have given the Big Picture, check for understanding. This can be done in various ways. One method is to use the 'Traffic Light' system where the children are asked to equate their level of understanding to a traffic light. Green means 'I understand', amber means 'I'm not sure' and red means 'I don't understand *yet*'. For the youngest children this could be simplified and only the red and green lights used. Once you are sure that all the children understand what the session will entail, you can move on.

Assess the starting point. This ensures that the session builds on what has gone before. Getting input now from children allows the practitioner to connect their ideas to previous experiences and draw upon their current knowledge. Each child has some sort of prior understanding that he or she brings to an experience. Every starting point is different. For example, when Samantha's teacher begins a literacy session on *Cinderella,* Samantha and George bring very different understandings to the session. Samantha went to see *Cinderella* at the pantomime last Christmas. The story was somewhat untraditional, and her memory is predominantly of bright lights, lots of laughter, and an exuberant dame getting dressed to go to the ball. George has a copy of the book at home. He just remembers the Ugly Sisters trying to squeeze their ugly toes into the shoe!

Deliver the session in chunks through VAK. It is essential that practitioners break the longer sessions down into smaller parts, giving attention to the transition between activities. The crude rule of 'age plus or minus one minute' can be used for gauging children's attention span. This means that a four-year-old might have a focused attention span of between three and five minutes, whereas a five-year-old's attention span might be between four and six minutes. But, of course, there is no substitute for a practitioner's judgement as to when children are wandering off task! Sessions should be planned with VAK (visual, auditory and kinesthetic learning) in mind, in order to cater for the varied learning styles of individual children.

Build in brain breaks. For young children physical movement is essential for learning. Brain breaks can be planned or spontaneous. For example, in this session the reception teacher leads the children in role-play activities to break up the session. At one point, the children get down to scrub the floor and experience Cinderella's despair. At another point, they struggle to fit on an imaginary shoe that is three sizes too small. These brain break activities serve two purposes: they provide opportunities for physical reprieve, and they enrich the experience of the children.

Check for understanding and acknowledge achievements. Throughout the session you will have been observing and assessing children's understanding and progress. Now is the time to clarify and consolidate your findings, and to acknowledge what has been achieved. This may be by simply discussing what has been learned with the group or with individuals. Or it may involve one practitioner making a note of what is said as another questions the group. After the session, the team may wish to have a more formal discussion about their observations and maybe enter the information on children's records. The most significant children's individual and group achievements should be briefly acknowledged here, with maybe taking a moment to celebrate with a bow or a clap or a 'well done' song.

Review the session. Review should take place naturally and continually – at the end of activities, at the end of more formal sessions, at the end of the morning, at the end of the day, and at the end of the week. Reviews should never become a chore – they should be kept short and be enjoyable for both adults and children! Each review should contribute to the ongoing To Do list in the classroom.

Step 4: Talking the language of learning

The language of the child

One of the most influential pieces of research on the language and learning of young children was that by Betty Hart and Todd Risley at the University of Kansas.[69] They found that:

> a child from an advantaged, educated home will hear something like 700,000 affirmations by age 4 – parents affirming: 'You're doing something an adult finds important and interesting.' A child from a welfare family will hear about 100,000 affirmations by age 4.[70]

The researchers measured the IQ levels of the children in the study and found that the parents' education, social status, race, or wealth were not as significant as the quality of language used within the home. While the definitions of 'types' of families in this study may be somewhat contentious, the results are quite clear. There are wide differences between the amount and quality of language that children experience, and the impact of this exposure to language will affect levels of attainment.

The quality of interactions that a child has, both at home and within the setting, impacts on his set of beliefs about himself as a learner, which in turn impacts on achievement. The nature of the child's talk will often be the deciding factor about how effectively the child learns. The practitioner needs to take care not to 'talk down' to children who might seem less articulate because they are less socially comfortable than some of their peers. She needs to take time to listen to how children interact with their parents and carers. She needs to intervene when she hears negative self-talk and to work to foster positive interactions and attitudes towards learning. In short, positive self-talk leads to positive learning.

Fostering positive self-talk

Using explicit language about desirable behaviours and qualities is the key to helping children to use that language for themselves and about themselves. Language gives power to positive thinking. In a roundabout way, when explicit comments and affirmations are used about positive attributes, the behaviours often change to

fit their new descriptions! Think about the power of the comments, 'Carrie, you are such a gentle girl. Jonah was so lucky to have you there to help him up when he fell off the bicycle' or 'You are always so kind, George. Thank you for carrying my heavy bag all this way.' Being explicit about such qualities gives children the vocabulary to describe themselves positively.

One practitioner played games where she made badges for children to wear that were printed with positive adjectives about themselves. The group would discuss the meanings of the adjectives before starting work, and she would reinforce the meanings through the day. 'Jomoke is cutting out her picture so *carefully*,' she would comment, 'that's why her badge says "careful Jomoke".' Gradually the children began to incorporate these adjectives into their own vocabulary, and would make positive comments about themselves and their friends.

For some children, intensive work has to be done to rebuild damaged self-esteem. It is the adult's responsibility to find creative and explicit ways to constantly 'talk up' achievements for these children. One teacher used circle time to create opportunities for children to say positive things about themselves. She called this the 'Blow your own trumpet' game. The children would hand around a trumpet, and after giving a good blow on it, would have to tell the group something that they had achieved that day, or something they most liked about themselves, or something that they believed they would achieve soon. The teacher found that as the children became accustomed to the game, they became less self-conscious. Eventually they would 'blow their own trumpets' at other times, and would accept positive compliments about themselves without showing discomfort.

Here are more ways to help children to develop positive self-talk:

 At the start of a session, talk about the qualities that would ensure success.

 At review time, reflect on the reasons for children's successes.

 Write stories and accounts of the positive things that happen during the day.

 Make connections to children's individual personalities when reading stories.

 Display photographs with captions to record positive events.

Pole-bridging

One of the most effective methods of enriching and accelerating learning is called 'pole-bridging'. Pole-bridging is talking your thoughts aloud, describing what you are doing as you actually do it. Young children do this quite naturally as they play, until they become aware that talking to yourself is not always socially acceptable! But pole-bridging is a valuable skill that should be encouraged.

When Carrie pole-bridges, she needs to pay close attention to what she is doing. She needs to find the language to fit the experience by noticing details, hypothesizing, analysing and reflecting. Linking language to the experience helps her brain to lay down neural pathways. Connections are made between the language sites and other areas of the brain. When this is practised repeatedly, the connections become stronger and the neural pathways are laid for life. Imagine a jumble of telephone wires connecting houses together all over a city. As more and more traffic travels along the most popular routes, the wiring has to be made wider and stronger. That is what is happening to the important pathways in Carrie's brain.

Today Carrie is pole-bridging as she plays in the sand pit.

Pole-bridging is helping Carrie on the way to becoming metacognitive. Metacognition is when you are not simply aware of what you are learning: you are aware of *how* you are learning. This is one of the most valuable aspects of self-knowledge for effective learning.

The language of the adult

 A teacher affects eternity; he can never tell where his influence stops.

Henry Adams, American author, 1838–1918

The Thinking Child · Brain-based learning for the early years foundation stage

Keeping it positive

The language that is heard by young children is probably the greatest influencing factor upon their self-esteem and motivation. Think about the difference between 'Amrit, walk. We don't run on the stairs!' and 'Amrit, I was telling Mrs X how beautifully you can walk down the stairs.' There is a magic about making positive statements: children generally respond by displaying the positive behaviour that you describe, rather than the negative one that might have been their first inclination! Using a calm, positive tone can often redirect a child from a primitive 'fight or flight' response, helping her to 'regroup' and make a more measured, reasonable choice. One special needs teacher used the words, 'about to' with her group of very challenging children. 'I'm so pleased to see that David is about to sit in his chair,' she said. David, who until then had very little intention of sitting in his chair, looked at her in surprise and sat down in his chair!

It is important to be vigilant about how you respond to boys as opposed to girls. Research shows that boys often behave differently from girls, even when the practitioner does not perceive this to be the case. A QCA study into boys' underachievement in English found that when given a choice:

> *From a young age, boys choose to spend more time on activities which do not involve adults, and this affects the nature of their relationships with teachers and helpers. In general, boys prefer active pursuits and may find it harder to acquire the more sedentary skills of reading and writing.*[71]

The researchers found that one of the keys was for teachers to work hard to engage the boys in active learning:

> *Boys respond well to clearly set tasks with well-defined outcomes. Boys respond to strong and enthusiastic teaching.*

One strategy for avoiding the gender trap is to ask a colleague to keep count of the number and type of interactions that she sees you engaged in with boys or girls. She can keep a notepad in a pocket or attached to her belt, and tick under the 'Boy' or 'Girl' column whenever she notices an interaction taking place. She can also add a 'D' for giving a direction, an 'A' for using *The Three As*, or a 'Q' for asking or answering a question. An analysis will later show whether or not your teaching has a gender bias.

Good questioning strategies

Asking George a good question as he mixes the red paint with the blue and sloshes it over two well-glued cereal boxes, and all over himself, is a skill that many practitioners have down to a fine art. However, our instinct might be to ask why on earth he was painting the box before it had a chance to dry, or even worse, to ask him to go and wash his hands quickly before he covers the rest of the clean table with his gluey painty mess!

It sometimes helps to pause for a moment and put yourself in George's shoes. George hasn't yet discovered that a thin smearing of glue will do the job better than his ample application, and besides, spreading glue is hugely satisfying. George also doesn't realize that if he covers the glue with wet paint, the boxes will most likely slip apart and will not stick at all.

George's key person stands back for a moment to observe what he is doing. She notices how he deliberately takes the blue brush and layers blue paint over the red, and she conjectures that possibly he has learned that when he mixes red and blue paint he has made purple.

Here is a model for good questioning strategies:

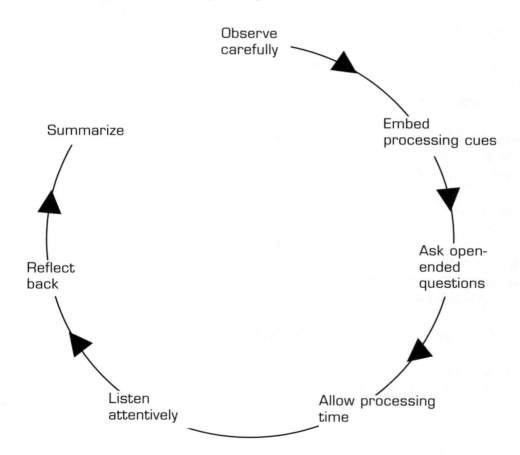

The first step to take when you are questioning a child about his learning is to *observe carefully* what he is doing or has done. Look beyond what is obvious. In this instance, the practitioner needs to look beyond the mess and notice how George is experimenting with colours. Next, as you go to ask your question, *embed processing cues* to help the child to absorb what you are saying. A processing cue gives the child time to process your question, for example, 'George, when you've put the paintbrush back I'd really like to ask you about the colours you mixed.' George has time to think about what he has discovered.

As you structure your question, make sure that it is *open ended*. An easy way to do this is to consider if the child is likely to give a one-word answer. If the practitioner asks George, 'Can you tell me about the colours that you were using?' George has many options open to him. The question allows him to tell her in his words what he discovered and opens the way to a more detailed discussion.

When you have asked your question, pause to *allow processing time*. This is especially important with the younger children. As a crude rule, the younger the child, the longer the processing time should be. This gives time for the child to absorb the question, formulate an answer and put it into words. Sometimes he may need to search for a word and, at this point, it is essential that he is not interrupted. The child is absorbed in his thought process, and silence is generally not uncomfortable to him, so avoid being tempted to fill in his gaps! This is when you need to give him your full attention and *listen attentively*. George told the practitioner that the blue paint kept running off the box, and she remained silent as he added, 'I couldn't keep it on!' She realized that this had been a source of frustration to him.

Next, *reflect back* what the child has said to you. 'That must have been frustrating, when the blue paint kept slipping off,' the practitioner could respond to George. 'Hmm, I wonder what we could do to make that paint stay on?' George's frustrations have been recognized, and together he and the practitioner can solve the problem. 'We could take some water out,' says George. 'How?' responds the practitioner. 'I don't know,' says George, and pauses, then adds, 'It can't.' 'No, it can't', agrees the practitioner. George shrugs. He doesn't have another suggestion.

The practitioner *summarizes* the discussion, and makes a suggestion. 'But you know what, to stop the paint being so runny, we could always add more powder to the paint!' she says. 'Do you think that might work? Would you like to get the powder and we could try?'

Giving effective feedback

Feedback should help the child to refocus if she is losing concentration. It should boost her confidence if she needs reassurance. It should help her to get back on track if she has lost her sense of direction. It should lead her to further learning if she has reached a plateau. It should reinforce positive experiences and help her to avoid negative ones. It should help her to deal with possible failure by embracing challenge.

A good model for ensuring that feedback is effective is to use the mnemonic of **POSITIVE**:

P ersonal – make it personal by using the child's name to preface your comments. Refer back to what she has achieved before.

O bjective – give the child an impartial view about her achievements. Make sure that your response is not influenced by your expectation of what she usually achieves.

S pecific – ensure that what you say is specific to that child and that activity by avoiding making generalizations.

The Thinking Child

Brain-based learning for the early years foundation stage

I nformative – give input that informs the child about what you notice she has achieved, and then help the child to think about what she might do next.

 T imely – give feedback at an appropriate time. This may be during an activity or it may be afterwards, but don't leave it too late for the child to still be receptive.

 I nspiring – inspire the child to want to find out and achieve more. Talk to her about how you might facilitate further learning.

 V aried – use different modes and styles for giving feedback: adult to individual, adult to group, adult to class, in front of the class or a parent, or quietly in private.

 E nthusiastic – show the child that you share her enthusiasm for learning!

It is tempting to make comments such as 'Well done' or 'Super!' during busy periods. But this is not educative feedback; it is simply a 'holding' exercise. A better model is to make short but meaningful comments, for example, 'That's careful colouring round the edges, Sam!' or, 'You glued that really securely, Avni.' Such comments take only a second or two longer but they have real meaning. This can be followed up later with more detailed feedback. The message given to the child is that the adult has taken time to analyse her work and appreciate her efforts. Her self-esteem is enhanced and she is likely to be motivated to build on her learning when she undertakes a similar activity.

This is an important purpose of giving feedback – the child should be encouraged to repeat the successful action or behaviour in similar contexts, or in more challenging situations in the future. Feedback should help her to clarify the learning that has taken place and make connections with what has gone before and what she might want to explore or attempt later. She should be encouraged by the experience to think more deeply and then be motivated to learn and achieve more.

For young children, it is important that feedback is given frequently during the experience or close to the experience. There is also value in revisiting what has been discussed during a feedback session some time later, when an activity is about to be repeated. Plenary sessions need to be built into the day to allow adequate time for feedback from practitioner to child, child to child, child to group, or group to group. During these sessions it is important that careful attention is paid to the balance of adult-to-child talk, and the balance of talk between the genders.

Feedback is a part of a learning loop:

Introduce
Give the Big Picture.
Explain the purpose of
the activity and describe
some possible outcomes

Establish the starting point
Find out what they already
know – through mind mapping
and discussion

Give time and status
to the **review**
of the session
(through discussion,
demonstration, open
questions)

Ensure you meet the
needs of different
learners (VAK)

Give feedback to help
with concentration,
clarity and motivation,
and **acknowledge
achievements**

Check regularly for
understanding

Deliver the session in chunks
Build in brain breaks and
movement

Plenary

Here are some points for reflection:

How might you want to re-organize any areas within your setting in order to implement any new techniques? Are there any areas that are wasted space? Are there any changes that you wish to make to your policy on display in order to maximize children's learning?

How good are the attention skills of the children in your setting? Do any children need help to improve their skills in 'good sitting' or 'good listening'? How might you do this?

What are the expectations within your setting for children's length of time on task? Are these appropriate demands? How might you help individual children or the group to improve their concentration span and listening skills?

If you did an audit of the language used by adults in your setting, how much of it would be positive? What about the language of the children? How might it be made more positive? How could you improve your skills in giving effective and positive feedback?

Where do we go from here?

When the language used in the setting is positive, the environment is organized for maximum learning, and strategies are in place to help all children to focus and develop good listening skills, the scene is set for successful learning.

There are some special techniques that can then be used within a play-based curriculum to make the learning even more effective and exciting. That is where we head in Part Three, where you will discover some specific brain-based techniques for learning.

Developing brain-based techniques

The Big Picture

In this section you will:

Step 1: Learn about mind mapping, discover how to teach children to map, and learn why mapping skills come naturally to young children

Step 2: Consider the importance of play and think about how to ensure that your setting provides a balance of different types of play for all children

Step 3: Read about recent research into the connection between music and learning and learn some practical ways to use music to enhance learning for young children

Step 4: Discover why movement is essential for learning and learn about the specific types of movement that enhance learning in the early years

Step 5: Read about the necessity of monitoring the use of technology, and consider the use of a wide range of technology in the early years

Step 1: Teaching children to mind map

What is mapping?

For the first time in the three and a half million year history of human intelligence, that very intelligence has realized that it can understand, analyse and nurture itself.

Tony Buzan[72]

Mapping is a skill that comes naturally to young children and is one of the most powerful tools that can be used to enrich and accelerate learning. A mind map is rather like a spider diagram or a flow chart. The key word – the topic – of the map is written in the middle, supported by a symbol or diagram if required. The map then develops from the centre outwards, with key words or symbols joined by lines or arrows to show the connections. The key words can be reorganized as ideas evolve, and colours and symbols can be used to represent certain categories. For example, in a map about animals the mapper might draw a green dot next to all farm animals and a red dot next to all pets. A dog might then feature in two places – as a working farm animal and as a pet, so it would require both a green and a red dot.

The map can be drawn and redrawn, or built and rebuilt. It needs to make sense to the mapper, who can talk other people through his map and explain the connections that he has made. Children find it easy to map. It is not a skill that needs to be taught as much as one that needs to be encouraged. Often mind mapping is referred to as 'memory mapping', but particularly in the early years it should be seen as a way to link ideas and concepts and engage thinking, rather than an aid to memory. For that reason, we use the term 'mind mapping' as opposed to 'memory mapping' in this book.

Young children are usually eager to describe in great detail, for example, a model that they have made. They often make complex connections, drawing together unique aspects of their lives and learning experiences. Mind mapping connects right and left hemispheres of the brain. When a young child creates a mind map, his brain is forming connections, which the adult then helps him to translate in concrete terms onto the map. Each stimulus causes electro-chemical activity and activates connections between different brain cells. If the child is asked to make a similar map on another occasion, some of the same pathways will be activated, along with some new ones. As the child's experiences build his understanding, the connective pathways will become more firmly fixed.

In one nursery class the practitioner made real-life 3D mind maps with her class. On the carpet area they mapped their understanding of the topic 'Toys'. Using real toys, pictures and props, they categorized the toys and made links between concepts. Strips of card were used to link ideas. For example, an area of the mat was dedicated to wooden toys. A picture of an old-fashioned wooden tricycle was laid in that area, along with some wooden beads, bricks and toy cars. The word 'wood' was printed large in the middle of these items, along with a picture of a tree. At the end of the activity, all the labels and items were put in a box. In subsequent sessions, the mind map was laid out in slightly different ways with further items added. Children could choose to recreate the mind map themselves as an activity during the day. Later it was copied onto paper and displayed.

Mind maps need to be displayed where they are easily viewed and accessible. As new ideas emerge, they should be written directly onto the map, or on a post-it note. When children are mapping, you can be confident that they are making connections and building new concepts.

Five steps to mapping

1 Gather the children on the floor in a semi-circle. Talk about the topic for the map. It is often easier to make your first map a hands-on 3D map, so write the topic on a big label and lay it in the centre. Draw a simple picture next to the word to show its meaning.

2 Now start to build the map by asking children what they can remember about the topic. Write the key words on small pieces of card, along with a symbol or picture. You may want to have a supply of pictures already prepared to use. However, be careful not to over-direct the activity – your aim is to engage the children in building the map.

3 Ask children to fetch items that illustrate their ideas whenever practical. For example, a toy cat or dog can be placed on the map, or a wooden brick next to a plastic brick.

4 Next, use strips of card or paper, or lengths of wool or string, or if you are outside, use playground chalk, to connect the ideas and link concepts. Encourage the children to get up and help to build the map, and to talk about what they are doing.

5 When the 3D map is complete, you can either dismantle it, or leave it out for children to work on through the day. You can draw it out on a large piece of card to be displayed and revisited. Alternatively, you might want to take a photograph of the map for the children to refer to. At a later stage you may wish to make the map again, in order to extend the children's thinking. The maps can form a useful part of your assessment of children's understanding.

It is also valuable to use mapping techniques to enhance your own practice, for example

for planning. Many practitioners are experienced in working this way, referring to these plans as 'brainstorms' or 'theme plans'. The value of mind mapping is that one area of the curriculum or environment does not become detached from the others. Links can be made between curriculum areas because the whole plan is on view and all practitioners can contribute. Items from the To Do lists can be incorporated, and when the map is complete the information can be considered in the light of the principles of brain-based learning, for example by asking which activities encourage a 'can-do' attitude, or how music will be used to enhance learning. Later the mind map can be used as a record of what has been achieved, linking into record-keeping systems.

Once mapping is being used comprehensively by children and adults in your setting, you can be sure that you are all working in the way that nature and evolution intended.

Step 2: **Adventures in play**

Playing with a purpose

 *Imagination is more important than knowledge. Knowledge is limited. Imagination encircles the world.*

Albert Einstein

Brain-based learning for the early years foundation stage

‘ *In their play children learn at their highest level. Play with peers is important for children's development.* ’

Early Years Foundation Stage 2008

‘ I like playing in the sandpit with Joanne and Antonio. ’

Jess, aged three

'I'm not sending her to nursery school,' exclaimed Joanne's mother, 'they never do any work. All they do is play!'

Joanne's mother does not understand that for young children play is work, and work is play. Piaget wrote about how imaginative play helps the child to rationalize and make sense of her world. Through this play she meets intellectual and emotional needs, and prepares for life as an adolescent, then as an adult.

Each of our four children shows a healthy interest in different types of play. Their preferences alter according to their current interests and levels of development, but they are all fortunate that they are provided with ample stimulation at home and in their various settings. Without the opportunity to explore their world through play, they would be likely to develop difficulties in forming healthy relationships.

Research on baby rats has shown that when deprived of play, the result is disturbed behaviour as adults.[73] This must lead us to wonder what the effects are on children who are denied play opportunities in their formative years. If Daniel Goleman argues convincingly that EQ is a more influential factor determining a child's future than his IQ, then play has to be recognized as the cornerstone of early years education, because it is the one single activity that provides simultaneously for intellectual and emotional development.

In his book *Building Healthy Minds*, Stanley Greenspan describes how, in order to reach a level of 'moral consciousness', a child has to understand that actions will always have consequences.[74] For example, when George is cross because another child took his bucket and spade in the sand tray, he knows that if he snatches them back and hits his friend, his key person will not approve. The next level of understanding would be to realize, when the key person points it out, that his friend would be upset if he hit him, although George might not care too much! Beyond this level of thinking, which comes for most children between the ages of four and five, comes the ability for George to put himself into the other child's position and be able to control his reaction, and even scale his response according to his desire for a specific outcome. He might decide simply to take

back the bucket and spade, which will annoy his friend but not cause a fight, or he might decide to take them back with a little push, just to convey the message that he's upset. At this level, George is making a conscious decision about his response. He is developing emotional intelligence, but needs guidance to ensure that he learns to make responses that are appropriate.

Our four children went through stages that are accepted as the norm for the development of play. As a tiny baby, Samantha's play began at the functional level, as she played with her hands or repeatedly banged two blocks together. Later her play began to have more purpose as it went through the constructive stage, for example when she pushed all the shapes from her shape sorter into a tissue box. Soon her play began to take on an imaginative element as she began to engage in dramatic play. Finally, by the time she started school she could play games with basic structure and rules, although the ability to take part in organized games is one that will take some fine-tuning in the years ahead.

> The five aspects of emotional intelligence are **self-awareness**, **management of emotions**, **self-motivation**, **handling relationships** and **empathy**.

BRAIN BOX

Getting the balance right

'*The EYFS requires providers to ensure a balance of child-initiated and adult-led play-based activities. Providers should use their judgement and their knowledge of the children in their care in deciding what the balance should be.*'

Practice Guidance for the Early Years Foundation Stage, 2008

Achieving the right level of adult involvement in play

Experienced practitioners judge when to become involved in play and when to let children take the initiative. It can be tempting to over-organize or dominate play. A balance has to be achieved where structure and enrichment do not become control and spontaneous play is allowed to develop. The practitioner's role is to observe, interact and provide for the development and enrichment of play activities. Sometimes she will need to join in the game; at other times she will simply observe and make a mental note of how she might be able to extend the learning. Occasionally she will need to intervene to help children to manage their emotions or actions within the game. Through this sort of play children develop physically, cognitively, emotionally and socially. There are many reasons for getting involved in children's play, for example to help children to play collaboratively, to model new language or vocabulary, or to offer ideas about how to extend the play.

It is heartening to read recent reports that practitioners throughout the UK are looking carefully at the amount of time they allow for child-initiated learning through play. It is equally heartening to read that proposed changes to the primary curriculum are recommending learning through play at Key Stages 1 and 2, which may reverse the trend to attempt to enforce learning without an appreciation that children learn best through play.

The intense pressures of testing, target setting, and the Primary Strategy for Literacy and Numeracy have led to demands being made to cut back on play. Time needs to be used to maximum effect, but 'wasting time' must not be confused with *spending time* on worthwhile non-academic activity! Children need substantial periods of uninterrupted time to become engrossed in their own play. This is essential if play is to develop and grow into real long-lasting learning. Researcher Jacqui Cousins, from the Oxford Brookes University, observed four-year-olds interacting with their teachers. She found that:

> *For most children, being stopped in the middle of the learning process was worse when little or no warning was given that a session was coming to a close. When such interruption occurred, I observed how seldom children were able to pick up the threads of their thinking or their action.*[75]

Intervening in play at the right moment is vital. Making the judgement of what is the right moment is a skill that can take a lifetime to perfect – and sometimes even the most skilled practitioners get it wrong! Being aware of the purpose for getting involved means that the practitioner can make a better judgement about when it is a good idea to join in the children's learning and enrich the experience, and when it is better to allow them to create their own adventures and follow them through to their natural conclusion.

It is no small challenge to provide adequately for children's play. This is an age where, sadly, marketers are working hard to encourage children to grow up faster and leave childhood play behind. This is a time of 'age compression', with children being encouraged to desire clothing, gadgets and toys that would in the past have been considered unsuitable for their age group. Companies work aggressively to create 'pester power' – where children wear exhausted parents down to the point that they will purchase inappropriate and expensive items. The book *Brandchild: Remarkable Insights into the Minds of Today's Global Kids and their Relationships with Brands* is written for an audience of business people who want to establish clientele within the 'tween' market – young, pre-teen children. Brand loyalty is sought from birth, and successful brands are carefully developed to appeal to this new, outwardly more sophisticated child. Children are turning their backs on imaginative play:

> *Girls, for example, are over Barbie at the tender age of eight. This used to be around 11 or 12. Boys of 10 are no longer interested in LEGO.*

Martin Lindstrom[76]

In a culture where children are being enticed away from healthy play, practitioners may need to explicitly teach them how to play with traditional toys. They also need to educate parents, carers and colleagues about the importance of play. One of the best ways to do this is to lead workshops where adults have to explore new concepts – through first-hand play experience!

Getting children outdoors to play

> *Outdoor provision is an essential part of the child's daily environment and life, not an option or an extra.*

Gail Ryder Richardson[77]

In an era where children spend increasing amounts of time engaged in sedentary play, it is encouraging that daily outdoor play has now become a statutory requirement for the EYFS. The outdoor area should be an extension of the classroom. There should be no fixed 'playtime' and the concept of 'play' versus 'work' should not exist. In the most effective settings, the outdoor area is used by groups of children, weather permitting, continuously throughout the day. Children come and go from indoors to outdoors, and themes from one area naturally extend across to others. For example, in one nursery class a group of children gardened outdoors, digging a new vegetable bed. Inside, another group of children were busy making a scarecrow to keep the birds from eating the seeds.

This type of imaginative use of the outdoor space should extend to stimulate every type of play. Some children choose to play outside, while others are more reluctant. It is important to help children to achieve a balance of different types of play, while recognizing that individual children will go through stages of preferring one type of play to another. If practitioners plan for indoors and outdoors together, it becomes easier to encourage children to take part in activities in both areas.

Tables can be set up for art activities outside, the home corner can be taken out of doors, and small world play toys can be set out on blankets in the garden. Themes can be developed for both indoors and outdoors. For example, the train set can be set out on a mat outside, while the big brick area can be set out to encourage children to build trains. If practitioners resist the temptation to think of either 'inside' or 'outside' activities, children are more likely to move from their comfort zones and take part in a wider variety of activities.

Almost all children like to spend time gardening. Digging, planting, trimming and watering plants are activities that have enormous learning potential. You don't even need a natural earthy area in order to create a garden: imaginative use of grow-bags and a variety of containers can give endless possibilities for gardening even in the most barren concrete jungle. A compost bin can be used for old leaves and trimmings, and children can take responsibility for saving and composting scraps left over from snacks.

The key to providing a stimulating outdoor environment for young children is not necessarily to have a great deal of money to spend. It is more important to have a great deal of imagination! If you have a difficult outdoor area to organize, you will need to use even more imagination. Look for ways to link the play from indoors to outdoors, such as by using the wheeled toys as pizza delivery bikes, or by having a car wash or a parcel delivery service. Brainstorm ideas with other practitioners and visit other settings to gain ideas about how others set up their outdoor areas. If you do not have an area for children to play outside, try to make use of the school or village hall, the local park or a games field where children can run and play with their whole bodies and in freedom. Children can help beforehand to load up a wheeled trolley with a selection of play items.

Inexpensive items can be collected for use to stimulate outdoor play, such as lengths of plastic guttering and tubing for water play, large chalks to make roads and other maps for small world play, and big cardboard boxes for building buses, trains, or whatever comes into the children's minds!

For settings without access to an outdoor area, it is now a EYFS statutory requirement that daily outings are planned. For some practitioners, this can present a challenge, especially during the winter. Organization and routines are essential if these outdoor trips are to be successful. It is a good idea to have a backpack or the buggy always ready with essential items such as spare clothes, wipes, sunscreen and bottled water. There is nothing worse than locking the door with your arms full, then realizing that there are no spare nappies in your bag! Older children can help to check and replenish supplies after each trip, so that you are always ready to go. Having routines about who carries what, who pushes the buggy and who holds hands helps children to feel calm and secure. Once you reach your destination, reminding children of similar routines and rules can prevent confusion. For example, try 'adopting' two or three places at the park where you always try to make your base. Give names to these places, such as 'the shady bench', or 'under the big tree'. When you arrive at the park, tell the children clearly where you are setting up base, 'Today we're going to put the blanket under the big tree'. In simple language, remind children daily of your rules for things such as taking off shoes, and remind them of areas where they are allowed to play.

Creative planning can help to make these outdoor trips exciting without having to keep going to different places. Obviously, if there are many open spaces within easy distance, it is great to use them. But if you are limited to just one or two places, try taking different items with you to give the children new activities to do when they are there, such as playground chalks, Frisbees, fabric bags for collecting rocks, or some paperback books for an outdoor story time.

> **'** I like riding on the big red bike. If Miss Connor says I have to wait my turn, I go on the blue one instead. It's almost as good but the wheels don't turn as fast. **'**

Jake, aged four

Step 3: Maximizing learning through music

> **'** My favourite song is 'Walking on Sunshine'. It makes my shoulders wiggle around! **'**

Joe, aged five

> **'** *Music speaks in a language that children instinctively understand. It draws children (as well as adults) into its orbit, inviting them to match its pitches, incorporate its lyrics, move to its beat, and explore its emotional and harmonic dimensions in all their beauty and depth. Meanwhile, its physical vibrations, organized patterns, engaging rhythms, and subtle variations interact with the mind and body in manifold ways, naturally altering the brain in a manner that one-dimensional rote learning cannot.* **'**

Don Campbell[78]

Since the release in 1997 of Don Campbell's book *The Mozart Effect,* companies have sprung up to supply educators and parents with music and materials that are claimed to increase a child's IQ. The 'Mozart Effect' was first discovered by Drs Rauscher and Shaw from California. They discovered that students who listened to ten minutes of Mozart scored between eight and nine points higher on a spatial reasoning test than those who did not listen to any music. They concluded that listening to Mozart helps to organize the firing patterns of neurons in the brain, especially those used for spatial–temporal reasoning.

Scientists can now use brain-imaging technology to study the way that different parts of the brain show increased electrical activity when the individual listens to music. Elaborate neural networks are formed in the cortex to process music. New activity is seen in the brain when the individual engages in musical tasks such as learning to play an instrument, responding to music with dancing or movement, or learning to compose music. The right and left hemispheres of the brain have to communicate to make sense of the musical experience. It has been found that the corpus callosum, which is the route for communication between the hemispheres, is often thicker in the brains of people who experienced musical training as a child. Other researchers have found a link between children's ability in musical sound discrimination and their reading ability.[79]

Rauscher and Shaw found in a later study that pre-school children who had piano lessons developed superior spatial–temporal skills than those who had computer training.[80] These skills are important for mathematical development, for example for understanding proportion and geometry. All this makes powerful ammunition for those who argue for providing a rich and varied musical diet for children in the early years. Don Campbell believes the evidence indicates that:

> *Learning about music can be just as important to a child's intellectual and emotional development as learning to the accompaniment of music.*[81]

The benefits of providing a creative musical experience for all children are obvious, but we need to be cautious about some of the claims and be wary of many of the commercial products on the market. The popularizing of the Mozart Effect has led to some great products, some mediocre products, and some that make rather remarkable claims. Not content with targeting the baby market with items claiming to increase IQ, companies are now marketing gadgets to pregnant mothers. One example is the *BabyPlus Prenatal Education System*®, which mothers wear in a pouch for two hours a day, playing sequential 'lessons' of sounds that resemble the mother's heartbeat to the baby in utero. Apparently, babies who are exposed to these prenatal lessons demonstrate 'earlier developmental milestones, enhanced intellectual abilities, longer attention span, improved school readiness, and greater creativity and independence', although one wonders how exactly this could be proved to be true. One also might wonder what is wrong with a baby listening to its mother's heartbeat at its regular pace in utero, just as nature intended!

There is no doubt that music is a valuable part of our human existence and that it influences our mood and our ability to undertake challenging tasks. While experts argue as to whether it actually increases intelligence or simply mood and performance in tests, it is indisputable that the lives of children are enriched if they are introduced to a variety of types of music at a young age. There are many opportunities to utilize music for many different purposes, beyond the usual timetabled or organized music sessions. Music can be played to create the right atmosphere for various times of the day. For example, you might want the children to arrive in the morning in a calm, reflective mood. Or you might want to energize them after lunch, or help them to relax at the end of a hot summer afternoon.

Children thrive on familiarity, so some pieces can be used repetitively for specific purposes. For example, music can be used to indicate that it is time to begin or end an activity. Some practitioners use the same calm piece of music each day for snack time, finding that when children hear the music they go to wash their hands and sit down without needing verbal direction. Similarly, a familiar piece can be used to signal that an activity is coming to an end. A piece of music can also be used to demarcate the time that is needed to complete a task, while injecting a sense of fun to the activity, for example at tidy-up time or when putting shoes and socks back on after PE.

Music can act as a 'vehicle' for learning basic concepts. Parents have known this instinctively for many generations. Just think about how many of us still sing the alphabet to ourselves when flicking through a dictionary! Number songs and rhymes are an essential part of the early years experience and should be included in planning to ensure a wide breadth and variety of material. Some reception teachers start numeracy sessions with a 'maths to music' session where they sing number songs, rhymes and maths songs to well-known tunes, or use CDs or music downloaded to an MP3 player.

Learning nursery rhymes and songs has also been shown to have an impact on later literacy development. The phonics programme *Letters and Sounds* stresses the importance of providing this rich musical and linguistic experience for children in the early years:

> *Good teaching will exploit, for example, the power of story, rhyme, drama and song to fire children's imagination and interest, thus encouraging them to use language copiously.*

Letters and Sounds, DCSF, 2008

Variations of popular songs and nursery rhymes can be used with young children to help to give structure to routines, and even to help to maintain a cheerful atmosphere while doing chores! For example, one nursery nurse used this adaptation of the song *There was a Princess Long Ago* to make tidy-up time go with a swing:

We are the helpers in this room, in this room, in this room,

We are the helpers in this room,

In this room.

In this room.

Then,

We put the aprons on their hooks

We put the bricks back in the box

We put the tops back on the pens – and so on!

Finally, music can be used to increase the sense of joy when celebrating the children's achievements. One practitioner used Louis Armstrong's *What a Wonderful World* as a background for a regular Friday afternoon celebration. The children knew that when they heard the song begin, they should get ready to congratulate one another on a great week's work.

As the children in your care engage in exciting learning adventures, their experience can be made all the more exciting and enriching through the imaginative use of music. When movement is added to the experience, the learning can be even more effective. Using movement to enhance and accelerate children's learning is what we move on to consider in the next chapter.

Fascinating Fact

Even plants prefer classical music! A researcher from Denver conducted an experiment with five greenhouses of plants to see if music affected their growth. After several months, the plants that had listened to Bach and Indian music were thriving, and the vines even grew towards the speakers. The country-western listening plants were almost identical to those in the greenhouse that had no music. Sadly, the plants in the rock 'n' roll greenhouse did not do well; there were fewer flowers and their growth was poor.[82]

Step 4: Teaching and learning through movement

> *The more closely we consider the elaborate interplay of brain and body, the more clearly one compelling theme emerges: movement is essential to learning.*

Carla Hannaford[83]

The young child needs to interact with his world in a physical way in order to make sense of it. The early years curriculum should provide the opportunities for freedom of exploration and movement. The amount that a young child will move during a day can be staggering. An Olympic athlete once described an experiment where he was asked to 'shadow' a two-year-old for a day. By the end of the day he was more exhausted than after a full day's training at the athletic track! He could not believe how many miles a toddler could cover – at top speed – in a day!

Three-, four- and five-year-olds have developed a longer concentration span than a toddler. By this age, most children are capable of learning when and where it is appropriate to move or to sit still. As children mature, the demands upon them to stay focused can gradually be increased. However, movement still needs to be built into sessions where children are required to sit and focus. There are several reasons for this.

Each of us learns through a variety of strategies. These can be crudely categorized into three types: visual, auditory and kinesthetic, or, 'seeing, hearing and doing'. It is this 'doing' part that involves movement. You can probably picture a child with a strong preference for kinesthetic learning. He or she is the one who will typically fidget during quiet times; wanting to be the first to get hold of a musical instrument or hold the props for circle time. He or she will generally be found participating in exploratory, practical activities. Rarely will the kinesthetic child choose to sit and listen to an adult's explanation or watch a new skill demonstrated, preferring to have a 'hands-on' experience.

There are also physiological reasons why movement should be built into each session through regular brain-break activities. Aerobic movement increases the oxygen supply to the brain, which uses about one-fifth of the body's oxygen supply. Movement also reduces stress, which increases the amount of cortisol in the system. Cortisol is not useful if we want a child to be in a calm and positive mood for learning. In addition, exercise seems to increase the body's production of *neurotrophins*, which stimulate nerve cell growth and increase neural connections.

Movement can enhance activities such as helping children to write their names, form letters correctly or spell simple words. The phonics programme *Letters and Sounds* incorporates movement into many of its activities,[84] while the foundation of other programmes such as *Jolly Learning* is the linking of organized movements to concepts.[85] Children enjoy writing their names in the air with their hands or with a magic wand, or even a silly prop such as a carrot! They should be encouraged to write slowly with left hand, right hand and then both hands, with their eyes open and then with their eyes closed. As a fun variation, they can then write with their feet on the floor in front of them. Adding movements to songs and rhymes aids language development and the understanding and recall of new vocabulary.

There is evidence that specific types of controlled, organized series of cross-lateral movements can help with learning by connecting both hemispheres of the brain and strengthening neural pathways. This type of movement, known as 'Brain Gym'®, is described in the book *Smart Moves:*

> *Cross lateral movements, like a baby's crawling, activate both hemispheres in a balanced way . . . Because both hemispheres and all four lobes are activated, cognitive function is heightened and ease of learning increases.*[86]

Brain Gym® activities focus on specific aspects of sensory activation and are designed to activate full mind and body functions. Practitioners who use Brain Gym® talk of significant improvements in children's concentration levels, receptiveness to learning, and specific motor skills. Examples of Brain Gym® exercises for young children are cross crawling, the energy yawn or arm activation. At cross crawling, for example, children stand and alternately raise their left knee so touch their right elbow, and then their right knee to touch their left elbow. This is not as easy as it sounds! This can be done at different speeds and little 'skips' can be added between each set, and coloured stickers on opposite knees and hands can help. Other children might need individual support to join in, or for some children with additional needs, the exercise can be adapted as appropriate. Music can be added to energize and give a real sense of fun.

Brain Gym® exercises can be timetabled for specific short brain 'workouts' during the day, or they can be used simply as fun time fillers such as when waiting for snacks to be ready. It can be useful to create a space in your planning format to make a note of the exercises that you plan to use each week. You might wish to adapt the exercises. Popular children's songs can be adapted for brain exercises, for example, 'Heads, Shoulders, Knees and Toes', 'Pat-a-cake', 'Tommy Thumb' or 'I'm a Little Teapot'. Rhymes for gaining children's attention can also incorporate careful deliberate movements, such as:

Point to the ceiling (right hand)

Point to the floor (right hand)

Point to the window (left hand)

Point to the door (left hand)

Point to you (both hands)

Point to me (both hands)

And sit and listen

Quietly (hands crossed on chest)

Ironically, the importance of movement for effective learning is sometimes overlooked because it is so simple. It is easier sometimes to turn to more 'modern' techniques and equipment. That is where we head next in our learning journey: to consider the use of modern technology with young children.

Step 5: **The place for technology**

The appropriate use of technology

‘The best thing about the computer is when I get funny e-mails from Grandad with pictures on them.’

Evan, aged three

Real ICT for babies and children is active and interactive, with the child in charge of the object, not the other way around!

Andrew Trythall[87]

When we hear the word 'technology' in the context of education we tend to immediately think of high-tech equipment. The thinking in many educational circles is that young children should be provided with computer access, and certainly this is the current political agenda. Yet there are many other applications of technology that are appropriate for the early years.

Our purpose should be to help children to develop knowledge and understanding about the world, which includes a wide variety of types of technology, some of which we tend to overlook because they have become so familiar to us. The world for children today is very different from the world that we grew up in, and it will change even more during their lifetimes. It is our responsibility to help children to see the purposeful uses of this technology and to become competent in its use, without overlooking the essential skills and knowledge that enable them to operate independently of technology when appropriate. Put simply, if you have no concept of addition or multiplication, a calculator is useless to you. Balance, as always, is the key.

There are many ways to introduce children to ICT within the context of daily life without the use of a computer. One childminder taught her five-year-olds how to use a movie creator and the children spent hours filming the pet rabbits as 'movie stars' and narrating their stories in imitation bunny voices! Children can help to transfer photographs onto digital photo frames and choose accompanying music. Voice recordings can be made on dictaphones or recorders such as 'Talking Tins',[88] and children can learn to program musical keyboards and to set alarms and clocks for timed activities.

As part of a rich technological diet and used with discrimination, there is no doubt that computer technology can enhance learning. But an emphasis needs to be placed on balance, with some experts urging caution about using increasing amounts of technology with very young children:

> *While the "learning" gained there (e.g., knowing letters, geometric shapes, reciting the names and characteristics of all the dinosaurs) looks impressive to adults, it may be only superficial mastery. Children playing with unit blocks may not know the name of a "rectangle," but they have a gut-level understanding of its properties and how it works.*

Jane Healy[89]

Literacy expert and author Sue Palmer adds another voice urging caution to the temptation of blindly increasing computer access for children in schools:

> *When used merely to support a narrow, standards-driven school curriculum, there is scant evidence of computers making much difference to educational achievement.*[90]

The quality of software targeted at young children varies considerably. It is essential that practitioners look beyond the special effects or the 'cuteness' of software. Be cautious about programmes that give children immediate gratification for impulsive answering. Teddies that dance when a child gets the right answer may seem cute, but if she simply hits keys randomly in order to get the 'right' answer and trigger the special effect, her learning is negligible and, moreover, she is being rewarded for impulsive behaviour. Good software requires the child to take time to think before answering. Adults should use each piece of software themselves to analyse the learning that will take place when a child sits in front of the computer screen.

When the computer is used, its potential for extending thinking and learning needs to be exploited, with multiple uses being incorporated into daily life and with children being offered opportunities for meaningful interactions with adults. A study commissioned by the DfES, *Researching Effective Pedagogy in the Early Years*, found that computer use in early years settings is often limited to activities such as painting programs or for literacy support.[91] Adults generally gave technical assistance, and '*rarely engaged in scaffolding or interactions which encouraged sustained shared thinking during children's computing activities*'. Instead of managing the computer program, try opening up conversations just as you would at the sand tray. Kishan's teacher sat with him as he worked on a maths program, commenting, 'You gave the dog a red collar.' Kishan turned to her and started describing his uncle's dog, then turned back to select matching red items for the dog on the screen. The discussion moved onto how to mix colours. Later, the teacher found some books about dogs. The next morning, the children experimented laying sheets of coloured cellophane over pictures of dogs to see how new colours could be made. Cross-curricular links were made and Kishan's learning was extended.

Thinking of technology widely increases its usefulness tenfold. For example, when a teacher was talking about a book she was making about grandparents, one of the children commented, 'I don't know how old my Grandma is.' The teacher suggested, 'How about we email Mummy? She might be able to answer our question right now!' Sure enough, the mum sent an email back giving the information that the child wanted. Later, they searched the internet for historical pictures of their town. In another setting, children checked library books in and out on the computer, and a web-cam was used for 'teleconferencing' with children at another setting. A parent spent a Saturday afternoon on a ladder, setting up the same web-cam for children to watch baby birds hatch in a nest in the eaves of the school!

Children should always be supervised closely by an adult when using the internet.

With the current move towards inclusion, practitioners are becoming familiar with many types of ICT support for individual children with additional needs. Some of these will be specialist equipment such as interactive communication aids, switches and electronic equipment especially programmed for the individual child. Other equipment such as talking photo frames, specialized keyboards, and sensory equipment might be suitable for use with the whole group. It can be valuable to use sensory equipment for the whole range of abilities and needs, as a multi-sensory environment can help all learners.

Children's exposure to technology will naturally vary enormously, from those children who are frequent computer users, to those who have little experience with any forms of technology, and all shades in between. The responsibility of practitioners is to ensure that they offer a healthy technological 'diet'. The key has to be to find a balance, so that technology takes a rightful place in helping children to develop knowledge and understanding of the ever-changing world in which they live.

The management of computer use

> *We simply need to appreciate that common sense is never out of date. Good judgment tells us that children need to be introduced to this exciting new world at their own time and pace and in keeping with their developing abilities and interests.*

David Elkind[92]

If you were to ask, 'What is the biggest challenge for you in managing ICT in your setting?' it is most likely that many practitioners would answer, *'The computer'*. Often, the answer is to simplify and organize what you have, rather than add more items. There is nothing more frustrating than computers that regularly crash, or a hotchpotch of software that doesn't match the children's needs. A good rule of thumb is to have fewer pieces of software, but make sure that they are good quality.

For many practitioners, the difficulties in managing ICT can be reduced by brainstorming practical solutions to questions such as where to place the machine, how to manage the software, how and when to provide internet access, how to supervise and monitor children adequately, and how to ensure that all children have fair access to the equipment. It is very important to consider the issue of gender bias. It has been shown that boys come to dominate computers in the classroom from the earliest age. Research by Bergin et al. in 1993[93] found that when grouping young children at the computer, boys invariably dominate the activity, even though at this age girls are as interested in computer activities as boys. Then, as girls get older, their interest declines, suggesting that the school experience perpetuates gender bias.

It is wise to have a clear policy that ensures that the use of computers in your setting enhances both learning and learning attitudes for all children. Consider questions such as:

What does the software that we use offer to children's learning?

How does our software encourage good learning attitudes?

How do we select software? How do we monitor its success or otherwise?

Has each practitioner used and evaluated each piece of software?

Does any of our software reward impulsive behaviours?

How do we ensure that there is equal computer access for all children?

How do we ensure that adults interact meaningfully with children on computers?

But the fundamental philosophy that can allay many concerns is that a computer should not be the focus of ICT. It is just one tool to be used, integrated into the curriculum, and not a curriculum area or activity on its own. While half the children might use a particular piece of software one week, it doesn't matter if the other half does not. They can gain the same skills through a different computer activity at another time, or through an activity with blocks and Lego® bricks, saving the computer for another topic, another activity, another day.

Computers can be exciting and can enrich children's lives. But inevitably, sometimes they go wrong. When you sort out a computer problem, make sure that you give clear 'can-do' messages. Verbalize what you are doing as you troubleshoot, so that children learn from your example. Use correct language such as, *'Hmm, the cursor seems to have stuck.'* If you can't solve the problem, switch off, and tell the children that you will look at it later. Meanwhile, they can find a different way to do the task that they were attempting – like write a letter instead of the email, or get out the blocks to build a house or work out a maths problem!

The dangers of information and emotional overload

In this day and age, the information available from technology can lead to overload – for children as well as for adults. In the past, children grew up with little awareness of the world beyond their home and community. Television and the internet have changed that, and now many children are graphically exposed to the realities of the darker side of human experience. Unsuitable television programmes are now available at any time of day or night. The internet is available 24 hours a day. Reality shows are more popular now than high-quality drama programmes, and children are exposed to adult themes that would have been unthinkable 20 years ago.

Surprisingly, programming that is intended to be educational can, in its own way, also be inappropriate for young children. With the advent of video and DVD, came many wonderful nature and science documentaries, with amazing footage and high-quality commentaries. Many children's television programmes and websites have appeared with the theme of conservation and care of the planet. Of course, it is important to raise children's awareness of environmental issues. But this needs to be undertaken with reference to the level of understanding and emotional maturity of the audience.

At a discussion group, a parent told how her four-year-old son had nightmares after watching a children's television programme about outer space. After several disturbed nights, she realized that he had become terrified that an asteroid might crash into the earth, obliterating him and his family. Another mother talked of how her daughter becomes distraught whenever she hears any mention of the word 'endangered'. Her child feels helpless at her inability to save the planet.

The world has become smaller. In the past, children were shielded from frightening concepts by the fact that they were not yet literate. In this day and age, children are bombarded with information about the environment. Reputable educational websites offer games with a clear mission of raising children's awareness of environmental issues. No longer do children match the bunny to a hutch – they put the endangered giant pandas back into their forests.

This gives a sense of immediacy that removes the sense of distance: the rainforest can become conceptually as close to the child as the next city, and the future of the endangered tiger can seem as personal as the wellbeing of the school's guinea pig. The result is not necessarily a more environmentally aware and responsible generation: it can be a stressed, anxious one. We could be raising a generation that feels helplessness instead of empowerment, and that ends up with a sense of disconnect because their environmental education is coming from technology instead of actually being out in the environment.

In an article for the journal *Young Children*, researcher Nancy Rosenow argues that instead of discussing serious environmental issues with young children, we should be taking them outside to dig in the garden:

> *Hearing about major environmental problems at an early age can send the message that the world is a frightening and dangerous place. Help children learn to love the earth first by providing positive, meaningful, hands-on experiences, like watering trees or growing flowers. This can help children become the next generation of environmental stewards.*[94]

There are many ways to teach children about the environment, for example involving them in creating systems for recycling and reducing waste, teaching them to switch off lights, or creating a rainwater collection system for watering the garden. Providing these sorts of activities empowers rather than frightens them.

Responsible adults are aware of the need to set limits on the use of technology. But it is time to become more selective about the 'educational' material that children are exposed to. We need to be critical of all resources that we draw upon, even those that appear to be the most worthy.

Plenary

Here are some points for reflection:

How could you use mind mapping in your everyday life? Have you noticed any ways that children naturally map ideas and make connections? How could you go about encouraging the children in your setting to map their ideas and findings?

Is there a balance in the types of play in your setting? Do the children use the outdoors as freely as the indoors? How could you rectify any imbalance? How do you ensure that there is a balance between adult-initiated and child-initiated play?

How do you already use music in your setting? Are there ways that you could expand your use of music to enhance learning? What resources might you need? How could you introduce new ways of using music for specific purposes?

Do the children in your setting get adequate opportunity for movement? Are there times when they are expected to sit for sustained periods? Do some children find this difficult? If so, how might you help them?

How extensively do you use technology in your setting? How do you evaluate the technology diet that is on offer to the children? Do you interact meaningfully with children when they use the computer? How do you protect children from technology overload?

Where do we go from here?

Once the specific brain-based techniques such as mind mapping and using technology, music and movement for learning are incorporated into a stimulating and balanced play-based curriculum, the potential for children's learning is greatly enhanced.

The teaching and learning can become increasingly creative, and it can be moulded to suit the different types of intelligence and learning styles of each unique child. This is what we will consider next: how to teach creatively for the individual children in each setting.

Part Four

Teaching for intelligence

The Big Picture

In this section you will:

Step 1: Find out about the research into the quality of learning through different teaching styles and be given many suggestions of how to be creative in your work

Step 2: Consider the importance of encouraging children to cooperate in groups and consider some different ways to organize group-work

Step 3: Read about learning through VAK– visual, auditory and kinesthetic – or seeing, hearing and doing, and discover ways to help each individual type of learner

Step 4: Learn about the multiple intelligences and discover how to recognize these forms of intelligence and cater for them in your setting

Step 5: Consider the pressure of modern life on children and read about the importance of providing for adequate relaxation and allowing time to hang out

Step 1: Creative teaching for better learning

An American researcher called David Weikart conducted an experiment in the 1960s involving two groups of children from poor neighbourhoods.[95] Both groups of children were educated through pre-school for exactly the same number of hours per week from the age of three to five. The difference was that one group was taught using direct instruction and rote-learning, whereas the other group was taught through active learning.

Albert Einstein[96]

My teacher does funny things to make me laugh. My dad makes me laugh too.

Eleni, aged three

At the age of ten, the IQ levels of both groups had climbed significantly, but there was no real difference in IQ levels between the two groups. Yet by the age of 23, significant differences had begun to emerge. Of the children who had been in the rote-learning group, almost 50 per cent had needed treatment for emotional problems, 39 per cent had been arrested for a felony offence, and only 27 per cent planned to graduate from college. Of the children in the other group, only 6 per cent had suffered emotional problems, 10 per cent had been arrested for a felony, but 70 per cent planned to graduate from college.

The significance of this experiment is that even if academic test scores can be shown to be equal after widely differing types of early years education, the importance of active learning stretches far beyond academic attainment into the realms of emotional and moral wellbeing. We now know that the actual process of learning is as important as the learning outcome. We understand the importance of play and of providing a stimulating and exciting environment where children engage in a wide variety of activities and experiences. One of the most exciting things about working in the early years is the fact that practitioners often have the greatest of imaginations and come up with endless ideas about how to make learning exciting and fun.

One nursery teacher developed what she called the 'fantasy classroom'. She would take a theme, such as a fairy tale, and develop a fantasy with the children within the classroom – quite literally pretending that the children and staff were taking part in the fairy tale. For example, on one occasion she built a bears' cave from blankets hung from the ceiling for the children to discover when they arrived the next morning. Torches and tiny flashlights lay

by the door to the cave, and the children gradually ventured inside, to discover three fluffy bears with wet noses sitting within the cave! The next day, when the children arrived at school they found a track of bear footprints leading from the cave to the outdoor area, and there, under a canvas cloth, were the three bears, sitting ready for a picnic. The children's play continued throughout the week as they expanded and enriched this fantasy, building furniture for the bears, making food for them, and even learning to talk 'Bear Language'.

By providing unusual activities and doing the unexpected, children's thinking can be challenged, causing them to need to draw on past experiences to make sense of the new. This is the most effective way to learn: to have a concept that is already held challenged by something new. When this happens, the child has to reconsider her current understanding of the concept and check it against new criteria. This may confirm what she already knew, or lead her to reject what she previously thought, or it might create a new level of understanding.

In order to make sure that the children in your setting are challenged by new and unexpected experiences, it can be helpful to simply move equipment and materials from one place to another, imagining how it might be used in a different context. When you are planning, take time to think about what could be done to make the activity a little more unusual. Consider how you could make an activity multi-sensory. What about adding scent to the playdough? Why not use unusual colours for the water tray: how would the children respond if the water were black or dark brown? What music could accompany an activity: how about composing a rap to sing about the *Three Little Pigs*? How could the paint be made more textured: how would the children react if you added sugar, or rice and glue to the paint pots? Get creative by putting the boats in the sand tray, filling the water tray with ice cubes or leaving a trail of strange footprints across the floor or on the path.

Children themselves are masters of original thinking. A pre-school leader told of a project that was started when Mimi, aged four, suddenly said, 'What do you think Jake-the-Peg did when he needed a new pair of wellies? How did he get enough wellies to go around all his feet?' Mimi and her friend experimented with a doll, who they called 'Jake-the-Peg', and several pairs of boots. As children engage in these unusual activities, encourage them to use language to describe their thinking. If they pole-bridge as they play, the experience will become more concrete and the neural pathways that are created will become stronger. Link each experience to other concepts that have been learned, and then plan what could be investigated later. Making a mind map in the plenary session, then revisiting it at a later time is one of the most effective ways to do this. Allow children to suggest further ideas for their To Do list, and so build upon their ability to think creatively and take charge of their own learning.

The brain-based learning environment is one that is never static. It is exciting and it challenges the thinking of adults and children alike. Original thinking is encouraged and celebrated. Children and adults learn together.

Step 2: Fostering the beginnings of group-work

' *A mind that is stretched by a new experience can never go back to its old dimensions.* **'**

Oliver Wendall Holmes[97]

The importance of group-work now commands a lot of attention in education circles. If children can learn to cooperate with peers in the early years, the skills can be set for lifelong learning. Studies have shown that the quality of language and interaction improves dramatically when practitioners use good group-work strategies. A study by Judith Watson from the University of Edinburgh in 1999 found that the increase in classroom talk could be as much as from 5 per cent to 40 per cent when teachers were skilled in fostering cooperative learning.

During the EYFS there is naturally a mixture of time spent in different types of groups. Much of the time the groups are self-selected, or simply occur through circumstance: if three children choose at any one time to play in the sand, then that group might engage in cooperative play. However, five minutes later, another child may join them and two of the original group may leave. The balance of time spent in different formations of groups will largely depend on the organizational aims of the practitioner. Sometimes she might gather together a specific group of children to take part in an activity, but at other times the group that evolves will be determined by the children themselves.

When we add into this scenario the fact that children will be passing through various developmental stages of play, we can see that the early years setting has numerous possibilities for group-work. As children pass through the various stages of play, they will first only engage in solitary play. Then they will begin to play alongside other children in parallel play, and then engage in associative play before finally being able to play cooperatively with their peers. This will not necessarily be a linear progression. All children in the early years will be at some stage on the continuum between playing alone and working confidently in a group, and it is the job of the practitioner to organize activities that help children to develop the strong social skills that group-work demands.

In George's pre-school, social skills are fostered through the children being given opportunities to become involved in the organization and running of the setting. In addition to the usual expectations of children to help to tidy the room at the end of the session, the staff find ways that the children can help with additional tasks. For example, when the staff decided to wash all the outdoor play equipment, they made it into an activity in which the children participated. George and his friends spent a very enjoyable and rewarding morning outside working with sponges, scrubbing brushes and water.

When a child is allowed to work on these sorts of real-life tasks, she often has no choice but to work in a group. With a practical task to do, the child has a greater incentive to cooperate with others. It is useful to comment on the skills needed to achieve a successful outcome, such as, 'Carrie, if you help Sam by holding the dustpan as he sweeps, he will be able to get all the woodchips swept up much more easily.' By being given explicit instructions on how to succeed, children can be helped to then transfer what is learned in one situation to another, such as, 'Good thinking, Carrie! That really helps Jimmy if you hold the bucket as he turns on the tap.' Other examples of everyday tasks that children  can be involved with include washing the home corner equipment, cutting flowers and arranging them in vases, sharpening pencils or preparing snacks.

Children benefit from working in a variety of group arrangements. It is important to ensure that each child has experience of different types of grouping. Each type of grouping creates different types of language and interactions. It is important to build in lots of opportunities for children to work in pairs with a friend. This helps to build a solid grounding for learning to work in a larger group. Sometimes it might be necessary to group children of a similar stage of development together in order to teach a specific skill or concept. At other times, encouraging pairings between a child who has a good grasp of something and another child who needs practice in that area can benefit both children: the 'leading' child reinforces what he already knows and can do, while the 'following' child learns naturally from somebody his own age. Sometimes, children benefit from working with a self-selected group of friends, while at different times it can be useful to randomly pick groups, for example by the colour or type of clothes that the children are wearing, or by hair or eye colour, or by giving out coloured stickers to children on the mat.

It will accelerate children's social development if you are explicit about the skills that are necessary for success in group-work. A useful model for teaching the more mature children to work systematically and reflectively is to teach them to use the 'Plan, Do and Review' model. Practitioners who use High Scope methods will know this system well. This requires children to take time to think and then verbalize their actions as they work. By working with the group to make a plan, the practitioner is helping them to learn to manage the moment of impulse – to resist the temptation to grab the materials and get started! The review session after the activity gives an opportunity for the group to reflect on the way that the group worked together.

Experience of group-work will enable each child to develop the skills necessary to work as a part of a team, which is a skill for success in all areas of life. Being able to work with two friends to produce a dinosaur out of the big blocks at the age of three or four is laying the foundations for being able to work with a team of technicians to make a major medical discovery 30 or 40 years later. The early years really are the start of a major adventure in learning!

Step 3: Teaching through VAK

Visual, auditory and kinesthetic learning

> *Learning is experience. Everything else is just information.*
>
> Albert Einstein[96]

> To have a good brain you need to be healthy and clever.
>
> Gaby, aged five

A simple way to explain differing learning styles is to break them down into three categories: visual, auditory and kinesthetic – in other words, seeing, hearing and doing. Each individual learner has a preferred style, but it would be simplistic to suggest that each person is a visual, auditory or a kinesthetic learner. Instead, we all have a preference for learning using one of these areas, but utilize all three methods to some degree.

Kishan is clearly a strongly kinesthetic learner. He likes to engage in physical activity, and is good at manipulating materials through three dimensions. By contrast, Samantha has strengths in auditory learning. Samantha listens well, and also finds it relatively easy to follow what her teacher is writing or drawing on the whiteboard as she gives an explanation to the group.

Each child has different skills, attitudes and aptitudes. The practitioner's role is to ensure that a balance is sought where there is an equal demand upon children's visual, auditory and kinesthetic engagement. The 'workshop' type of arrangement where there are clear guidelines for the different activities in each area can help to create this balance. The timetable also need to be monitored to ensure that there is a VAK balance. For example, story-telling sessions might suit auditory learners if CDs are used. However, if visual aids and props are added, the activity is more accessible to visual learners. If a balance of all three styles is offered over a period of time, then each child will be catered for and will have the opportunity to practise using each style of learning. As you monitor the balance of your curriculum, remember that some children have additional needs that require a different focus on specific methods of engagement. Some practitioners adapt their planning formats by adding tick boxes for VAK to ensure that they provide a balance.

Your personal learning preference will affect your teaching. Many practitioners find that it is helpful to analyse their personal learning style and that of their colleagues. You also need to analyse the strengths and weaknesses of the children, and encourage them to develop all-round learning skills. The more tools a child has under her belt and the more ways that she can approach learning, the more effective her learning will be.

Visual learning

At birth, sight is one of the least developed of all the senses. It has not been practised in the womb! Everything that is not between 20 and 35 centimetres from a newborn's face appears as just a blur. It is not a coincidence that Carrie's mother instinctively lent to gaze at Carrie's face at a range of 20 to 25 centimetres as she nursed her. Within a few hours of birth Carrie could recognize her mother's face. Research has shown that early visual experience actually affects the wiring of the brain:

> *The more a baby sees, and the better that input is suited to her visual ability at that particular stage, the better she is likely to be at the many later tasks that depend on vision. Who knows? It may even make the difference in whether she ends up as an artist, or a naturalist, or an expert tennis player.*

Lise Eliot[98]

Carrie does, in fact, have a strong visual memory. She amazed her mother before the age of two by saying, 'Home', whenever they were within a mile of their house, showing that she recognized familiar landmarks. She memorized the names of letters as a two-year-old and can now identify a few familiar words such as her name, her mother's name and some names of shops that she visits regularly. Of course, there is a balance of nurture and nature at work here: Carrie is naturally a strong visual learner, but her mother also supplied the environment within which Carrie could utilize this natural ability.

Practitioners now know that young children learn best within a play and exploratory type of environment, rather than from a formal 'instruction' model where the focus is placed upon the 'Three Rs'. However, it is important to introduce concepts such as letter and number recognition into everyday play activities. Carrie's mother did not actively 'teach' Carrie to recognize the alphabet, but she did give Carrie a wide variety of experience with

print, such as looking through junk mail and picking out the letters from her name, or pretending to 'read' cooking instructions. The result was that Carrie learned to identify letters and numbers naturally. Research shows that there is a correlation between children who can identify letters before entering school and later attainment in literacy, although of course it is important not to confuse this sort of stimulating, enriching activity with inappropriate formal instruction.

Strong visual learners tend to visualize situations before they engage in activity. They sometimes 'rehearse' a game in their mind, for example picturing what will be the outcome of a session in the home corner. They recognize patterns easily and can reproduce them accurately. They often repeat a previous experience by visualizing it first, for example arranging the small world toys in the same way as the day before in order to continue a previous game. They respond to visual prompts during circle or story time. They tend to remember experiences visually, and respond to photographs or pictures more readily than to lengthy discussions. Visual learners pay attention to detail in books, and remember visual details about experiences that others find it hard to recall, such as the clothes that somebody wore or the pattern that the snacks made as they were laid out on a tray. They easily memorize the tags and labels around the classroom and can identify other children's labels in addition to their own. These children usually grow up to learn to read whole words, often before gaining full phonetic understanding, and find learning to spell easy.

You can appeal to the visual learners in your setting by presenting information visually, encouraging children to picture what they are going to do before they begin an activity, and using language such as, 'How will the tractor look when it is finished?' or 'Can you imagine what will happen when we take this to the office?' By working in this way, you will also help the auditory and kinesthetic learners develop their skills in visual learning.

Auditory learning

'*If any type of prenatal stimulation is going to make a difference to a baby's mental development, it is auditory input.*'

Lise Eliot[99]

In contrast to vision, hearing develops early but matures slowly. The neural structures for hearing begin functioning well before birth, but are not fully matured until the child reaches school age. We know that babies at birth can often recognize familiar sounds and that they know their mother's voice almost immediately. We also know that the more high-quality language that children hear, the stronger their auditory and verbal development will be.

Samantha's greatest strength is in auditory learning. She enjoys story-telling sessions in the car with her mum and dad, and does not need pictures as an aid to concentration. When she goes to the supermarket with her mum she tends to maintain a running commentary as they shop.

Samantha is drawing upon her memory of a visit to Uncle Mark's house, triggered by the fact that her mother has put some fish in the shopping trolley. Whereas a visual learner might be picturing the memory, Samantha is talking it through, and needs her mother to help her to connect all her ideas successfully. Although her mother simply 'ums and ahs' through this conversation, she later brings up the subject in the car and helps Samantha to make sense of her memory.

Auditory learners have good listening skills and enjoy group story-telling, circle time and music sessions. They like to hear explanations and will often seek out an adult to talk to. They listen to answers and respond well to verbal feedback about their activities. They learn through language, and often engage in internal dialogue as they process their understanding. Pole-bridging often comes naturally to young auditory learners. If an adult joins in to provide verbal feedback and ask the right types of questions, she is maximizing the experience for the child with an auditory learning preference.

Auditory learners often like to engage in experimentation with language and word-play. They benefit from talking through an experience or activity, or listening to somebody else's description. Using language such as 'Tell me about your picture' suits auditory learners, along with specific comments about what they are doing, such as 'You've wound the string around the box and pulled it tight. Can you tell me what might happen when you cut it?' Plenary sessions are particularly important to auditory learners. Of course, this will also benefit the visual and kinesthetic learners.

Kinesthetic learning

' My dad says that I'm unstoppable on the climbing frame. '

Myra, aged four

Research has shown that exercise and physical movement is not just healthy for the body: it is good for the brain too. Yet the ability to learn through physical activity is often seen as being 'inferior' to learning visually or aurally. Howard Gardner challenges this perception by including 'Bodily-Kinesthetic' in his list of multiple intelligences.

Read about the multiple intelligences on pages 139–43.

Kishan is a strongly kinesthetic learner. He was an early walker and learned to climb onto the kitchen counter by the age of 14 months. From a very young age, Kishan always wanted to hold objects to explore them. He thrives outdoors where he can work with the big blocks, ropes and tyres, and he is often found out there working as chief engineer! Kishan can visualize how a construction will take shape and is good at manoeuvring the equipment through three dimensions.

Kishan is very agile, and climbs confidently on the most challenging apparatus. He enjoys setting out different arrangements with the climbing frames. He likes the dramatic aspects of stories, and loves to get up and do actions and move during story times. He often makes up actions to go with songs and rhymes. When his teacher describes a task, she often notices that Kishan is doing the actions that will accompany the activity. This is not conscious on Kishan's part: he needs to move in order to internalize information. He enjoys activities such as 'Body Maths', where the children actively represent mathematical concepts with their bodies.

Kinesthetic learners learn best through physical activity. They can present their parents with challenges in managing their behaviour – preferring to stand on the sofa than to sit to hear a story! They are well coordinated and are usually eager to improve their physical performance. This often leads to a competitive nature, where they enjoy climbing the highest apparatus, or riding the bikes the fastest or down the steepest slope. They demonstrate greater dexterity than their peers and have a strong sense of timing.

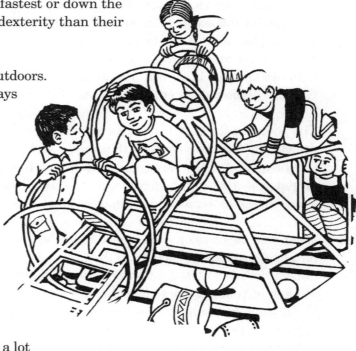

Kinesthetic learners often choose to play outdoors. The challenge for practitioners is to find ways to bring kinesthetic learning indoors, such as providing easels with marker pens for writing, large comfortable mats for small world play, and plenty of space in the book corner. These children find listening to stories easier if there are frequent breaks for movement or to shift position. Kinesthetic learners benefit from being encouraged to do actions to accompany a story. In music sessions they like to play instruments or clap or dance along to the music. This helps them to process the experience more fully. These children often need to be given a lot of help to develop the skills of 'good sitting' and 'good listening'. Breaking up sessions with brain breaks – short periods of physical activity – helps them to maintain their focus and develop their visual and auditory skills without feeling frustrated or losing concentration due to unrealistic expectations being made of them.

Now that we have recognized and provided for the three ways of learning, we can move on to consider a more sophisticated model for understanding intelligence – that of the multiple intelligences.

Step 4: Engaging the multiple intelligences

' *No problem can stand the assault of sustained thinking* **'**

Voltaire[100]

' *I was proposing an expansion of the term "intelligence" so that it would encompass many capacities that had been considered outside its scope.* **'**

Howard Gardner[101]

There are many theories about the nature of intelligence, with the most commonly understood and accepted being that of IQ. The problem with the IQ model is that it assumes that intelligence is a fixed phenomenon that is measurable through one test. It does not allow for the concept that intelligence can be increased through experience, nor does it allow for the idea that each individual possesses different types of intelligence. Howard Gardner offers a different model, that of the multiple intelligences.

The potential for bias in intelligence testing, combined with the idea that intelligence is something that one is born with (nature) and only somewhat influenced by the environment (nurture), makes the theory of 'multiple intelligences' a much more satisfactory model, although we do need to be cautious, as with all new theories in education, that we do not allow ourselves to make too simplistic an interpretation of the theory.

When new theories on intelligence are published, they can become popularized and influence education practices in the first rush of enthusiasm, without being really fully understood. After Gardner's work was originally published, it was followed by a large number of books, papers and recommendations of varying quality advising teachers about teaching using the multiple intelligences. Internet questionnaires now abound that supposedly tell you if you are linguistically or musically intelligent, or 'right-brained' or 'left-brained'. These can be interesting and fun, but should not be taken as scientifically accurate. What these exercises can do, however, is make us aware that all children learn differently and that we need to present them with a very wide range of experiences that incorporate music, art, movement and the outdoors. As the current educational climate demands more and more in terms of 'standards' in the basic skills, practitioners can use the multiple intelligence theory as a structure to ensure that the curriculum addresses the needs of the whole child and not just the demands of a culture of testing.

The eight 'intelligences' are:

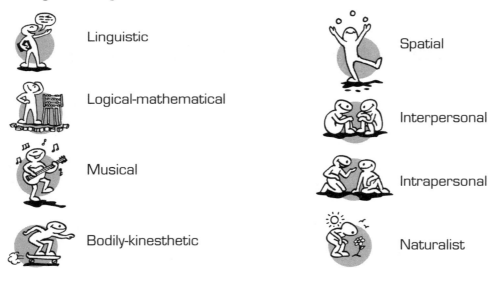

Linguistic

Logical-mathematical

Musical

Bodily-kinesthetic

Spatial

Interpersonal

Intrapersonal

Naturalist

The first two intelligences on the list are the ones that are most valued by our society and education system. If you are good with languages or a logical, mathematical thinker, you are likely to succeed in our culture. Yet who could deny that Mozart or Bach or John Lennon were 'intelligent'? Or any of the world's great athletes, or artists, or diplomats, psychiatrists, or biologists? When you move away from the limited thinking of intelligence being easily measurable and tested, and see the range of intelligences that exist in Gardner's list, the potential for valuing each child's potential increases dramatically.

How linguistic intelligence might show itself in a young child

A child with a strong linguistic intelligence will have an intuitive feel for language. He will usually speak early and his language will develop fast. He will have a good memory for new vocabulary and will make connections between words, for example realizing that 'desert' and 'dessert' sound similar but have very different meanings. He will experiment with sounds and rhymes and enjoy games such as making up nonsense words. The linguistic child will usually show a keen interest in the written word, and will enjoy stories and story-telling. He will learn the words to nursery rhymes and songs easily. He will pole-bridge naturally and uninhibitedly and will contribute to discussions enthusiastically.

How logical-mathematical intelligence might show itself in a young child

A child with a strong logical-mathematical intelligence will exhibit a strong memory for patterns and links. She will have an intuitive feel for what is orderly. She will often create patterns in her play, such as lining up the toy cars in order of size, colour or shape. She will notice when a pattern is broken. She will make links between ideas and experiences: if there were ten beads in one pot, how many will fit in this similar pot? She will automatically estimate and experiment. Problems will intrigue and excite her, and she will problem-solve enthusiastically. Her play will be organized and focused and she will apply her mathematical understanding from one situation to another.

How musical intelligence might show itself in a young child

A child with a strong musical intelligence will learn melodies easily and will be able to copy patterns. She will develop a good sense of pitch and rhythm at a young age. She will copy actions and techniques in music sessions and will often use her whole body when she responds to music. If given the opportunity, she will develop good technical musical skills, but even if she does not have this opportunity, she will have a natural 'feel' for music that cannot easily be taught. She will enjoy composing music and will hear 'tones in her head'. She will be uninhibited about singing and making music either spontaneously or in more formal group sessions.

How bodily-kinesthetic intelligence might show itself in a young child

A child with a strong bodily-kinesthetic intelligence will develop good motor skills at an early age. He will have an awareness of his body and its place in space. He will learn through physical activity and will usually be good at Brain Gym®. He will have a good sense of timing and be able to create and repeat sequences of movement. His movements will often be precise and he will take pleasure in repeating a movement and improving on it. He will often be a good mimic and be able to imitate other people's actions accurately. He will take pleasure in using tools and manipulating toys.

How spatial intelligence might show itself in a young child

A child with a strong spatial intelligence will be able to recreate scenes after the event, for example making the same layout with the small world toys the day after a complex game. She will be good at memory games. She will be able to visualize objects being rotated through three dimensions, for example when building junk models in the technology area. She will have a good concept of the layout of a room and will often be able to recreate a journey and recognize landmarks. She will usually have a good sense of colour and will be experimental in her artwork.

How interpersonal intelligence might show itself in a young child

A child with a strong interpersonal intelligence will play collaboratively at a young age. He will also develop a strong sense of empathy, often noticing other children if they are showing distress and showing signs of distress himself in response. He will alter his behaviour according to that of others and show sensitivity to moods. He will respond to books and stories about personalities and emotional issues. He will be anxious to have friends and will usually choose to work with others. He will enjoy tasks that demand a team approach and will usually be able to take turns and see other children's points of view.

How intrapersonal intelligence might show itself in a young child

The interpersonal and intrapersonal intelligences often go hand-in-hand. A child with a strong intrapersonal intelligence will therefore often display many of the characteristics of the interpersonal child. He will develop a sense of self earlier than many of his peers. He will be able to talk about his own emotions, and will generally be good at recognizing those of others. He will talk readily about how he feels and will often have a very strong sense of justice, causing him to sometimes seem intractable. He will respond thoughtfully to stories about dilemmas and feelings, and will want to relate fiction to his own personal experiences.

How naturalist intelligence might show itself in a young child

A child with a strong naturalist intelligence will enjoy being outdoors, especially in the garden, grassed or wild area. She will notice details about the natural world and will be enthusiastic about any activity that involves animals, plants or insects. She will categorize things and notice patterns and relationships. She will enjoy taking responsibility for plants or pets, and will show concern for the environment. She will enjoy looking at books about the natural world and may develop a deep knowledge about one or more aspects of wildlife.

Gardner's theory is that each individual person has an individual combination of these different intelligences. Each child has a combination of different intelligences in different strengths, and the environment will then influence how these different intelligences develop and flourish. It would be unnecessary and somewhat ridiculous to attempt to assess children against each of the eight intelligences. It would also be foolhardy to try to categorize individuals according to their intelligences. We certainly do not want children believing that they 'aren't a maths person' or 'are musically intelligent', and therefore deducing that they are not ever going to be capable learners! It is not wise to try sharing information about multiple intelligences with young children, but it can be a valuable exercise to think about which intelligences are a particular strength for each child. This can be done very quickly and easily, by making a list of the children, and drawing two columns down the side, one for each of the intelligences. You can then write S in the first column for children who you feel have a particular strength, and make notes in the final column as you consider each individual. Some practitioners ask parents to fill in a similar profile for their child, which gives an alternative perspective. It is interesting to also assess your own multiple intelligence profile, as your individual preferences will influence how you teach.

Whether or not practitioners in your setting explore the theory of multiple intelligences in depth, it is important that they recognize the fact that children have widely varying learning styles and so plan for a breadth and balance of the curriculum. An interesting Action Research exercise can be to create a checklist with eight boxes to refer to alongside curriculum plans. The researcher should then tick each box when a planned activity fosters that particular intelligence. She should then be able to see if any particular intelligence is being over- or under-emphasized in the setting. This can lead to greater creativity in planning ways to work with each unique child and monitoring of the curriculum, to be sure that a balanced range of activities is offered.

The effect of a curriculum that caters for the multiple intelligences is far-reaching. Children's individual learning styles and needs are catered for, and the curriculum becomes increasingly child-centred. Once the curriculum really matches the child's needs, he can be truly successful and his self-esteem flourishes. With increased self-esteem, his motivation to learn increases. We have provided an environment where practitioners teach *for* intelligence, and children learn *with* intelligence.

Step 5: Taking the time for learning

The pressure of time

We need the tortoise mind just as much as we need the hare brain.

Guy Claxton[102]

High-stakes testing can also blind teachers, parents and children to the importance of a wide and balanced curriculum.

Sue Palmer[103]

As life in the twenty-first century gets increasingly busy and the pressure builds for improved performance in schools, the temptation to hurry our children becomes harder to resist. The pressures of assessment and testing can lead to a pressure to 'do' more with the younger children to prepare them for the demands ahead. We can completely forget to stop to smell the roses because we are spending so much time dissecting them, teaching the names of their components, and doing art projects with the petals!

Children are now spending an increased amount of time in school and in other settings, and less time home in the family. Since the expansion in provision of school places for the early years, the proportion of three- and four-year-olds enrolled in schools has dramatically increased, rising from just 21 per cent in 1970/71 to 64 per cent in 2005/6.[104] Once all types of early years provision have been factored in, statistics show that by 2007 almost 100 per cent of four-year-olds in the UK attended some form of early years setting.[105] Many of these children also attend additional settings during the week, with some children spending part of each day in as many as four different locations.

In addition to time spent in early years settings, many parents often feel under pressure to sign their children up for organized activities at an early age. A child's small remaining free time can easily be consumed by sports, swimming, art, judo, music, gymnastics or dance class, not to mention time spent sitting in the car going from activity to activity. This leaves little time for play or creative activity, and still less time for thinking. The result can be a hurried child who is rushing to learn and grow up, all to the detriment of her emotional wellbeing. Parents are often manipulated into spending time and money on activities that in years past did not even exist. Author Pamela Paul describes many of these activities in great detail in her book *Parenting Inc.* She concludes that our modern lifestyle and the pressure of the media has left many parents frightened to resist the pressure to 'do' more with their children:

> *Guilt. Desire. Ambition. Insecurity, Expectation. Fear. Desperation. A prime marketing opportunity, and companies have met it.*[106]

The irony is that babies can learn as much from a walk through the park in a buggy or carried in a sling or backpack, stopping to look up at the trees and listen to the birds, than they would from going to a music class. Toddlers can do as much climbing and tumbling in the park or on cushions at a friend's house as they would do in an organized gymnastics class. Taking a baby or child for a walk or to the park eliminates the hassle and stress associated with attending scheduled organized activities and allows for a more natural 'flow' to the life of the child and carer.

It is not only adults who suffer from stress. There is a danger that many of our young children become stressed-out by the demands on them from a society that is expecting too much, too soon. Sue Palmer condemns the modern 'educational rat race', run along the lines of big business instead of education. She expresses great concern about this trend to rush children through childhood:

> *We wouldn't dream of suggesting twelve-year-olds should learn to drive
> (even though technically most of them probably could) because we know that
> emotionally they're not ready for the responsibility of being in charge of
> a car. Similarly, we shouldn't force unwilling four- and five-year-olds
> to struggle with skills most would learn easily a couple of years later.*[107]

Early years practitioners can help to stem the tide of this rush to over-organize children by reassuring parents that there is plenty of time for their child to learn to play the violin or tap dance or score goals in the future. Of course each of these activities is worthwhile and can enrich the life of an individual child, but a good piece of advice might be for a child to participate in just one such activity per week, with two being an absolute maximum. We can also encourage parents to allow for plenty of what author David Elkind suggests as an antidote for the stress of hurrying – play.[108]

A false perception – often fed to a frenzy by the media – of an extreme danger of child abduction has greatly aided the successful marketing of organized childhood activities, leading to a cultural obsession with 'child safety'. This has developed to a point where some children are not given opportunities to learn skills of self-reliance or develop independence. Instead, they are supervised closely and, directly or indirectly, taught to be fearful of the world. Author Gavin de Becker points out that many parents' favourite rule, Never Talk to Strangers, is both meaningless and counter-productive due to:

> *. . . the implication that people you know will not harm you. If stranger
> equals danger, then friend equals safety. But the opposite is true far more
> often . . . The irony is that if your child is ever lost in public, the ability
> to talk to strangers is actually the single greatest asset he could have.*[109]

The chance to mix with children of different ages and make up games from scratch, and to interact freely with nature – whether nature is the rural fields or the urban corner plot or allotment – is becoming a part of history rather than a part of childhood. In his acclaimed book *Last Child in the Woods*, author Richard Louv has gone as far as to say that this trend has created a 'Nature-Deficit Disorder' in recent generations of children:

> *Nature-deficit disorder describes the human cost of alienation from
> nature, among them: diminished use of the senses, attention
> difficulties, and higher rates of physical and emotional illnesses.*[110]

While we cannot change these twenty-first century facts of life, we can create some balance by ensuring that children are given the opportunity to spend long periods of time outdoors where they can interact with nature. This requires creative thinking. One nursery teacher noticed that a gardener was outside the school gates raking leaves into piles ready to remove them. She asked him to leave the piles instead. The next morning, she organized enough parents to take the children to spend an exciting hour diving into the leaves, throwing them around, and completely messing up the gardener's neat piles! Once everyone was exhausted, the teacher produced rakes and the parents and children helped gather the leaves again. For many of these children, this was the first time they had ever jumped in piles of leaves.

We can no longer take for granted that the simple pleasures that most of us enjoyed in our childhoods are still experienced by children today, yet they are essential if our children are to grow into healthy citizens with a true affinity with the natural world around them.

Rethinking the concept of 'dead time'

It is time to reflect upon the recent trend towards ensuring that there is no wasted time in schools and that every activity needs to be 'worthwhile' and 'purposeful'. In the light of the increasing pressure upon children to play less, 'do' more and grow up more quickly, it is time to reconsider our approach towards the concept of avoiding 'dead time' and utilizing every minute of time spent in the classroom. While children should, of course, not waste inordinate amounts of time waiting turns, it seems that children have become so scheduled that they have no time left, literally, to think! Thankfully, this was recognized in the 2009 final report of the Independent Review of the Primary Curriculum, which recommended a reorganization of the curriculum for Key Stages 1 and 2:

> *The availability of time and its management will continue to pose considerable problems unless a better fit of curriculum content to the capacity of primary schools can be achieved.*[111]

In the light of the sheer pressure on children, we need to become more attuned to recognize those times when they need to just 'hang out'. This might be together, or alone. It might be in a book corner, or at the top of the slide. It might be quiet, or it might be noisy. But not every minute of a child's life needs to be filled with an opportunity for learning. If we fail to provide time for children to relax as they process that learning, we may well be failing to allow them to learn.

Our drive to achieve more, and to do it at a faster speed, can lead us to fail to allow time for the sort of thinking that can really anchor understanding and allow for creativity, experimentation and further learning. In his book *Hare Brain, Tortoise Mind – How Intelligence Increases when you Think Less*, Guy Claxton points out that:

> *Many of those whom our society admires as icons of creativity and wisdom have spent much of their time doing nothing. Einstein, it is said, would frequently be found in his office at Princeton staring into space.*[112]

Practitioners need to take care that they provide time for this sort of unrushed thinking. Because we want to optimize the time that we have with the young children in our care, we can forget to allow them freedom to experiment with everyday materials. When people spend time experimenting they often come up with new, creative thoughts. If we never allow children time to experiment, we seriously limit the possibilities for learning.

We can also remove the joy of an experience by insisting that we discuss or record it. The teacher who allowed her class to jump in the leaves resisted the temptation to come inside to write poems or make rubbings of leaves. She was content to simply allow the children the joy of the experience. Claxton argues that if adults continually step in to have meaningful conversations with children, they are in danger of producing children who do not feel comfortable 'not knowing' everything. Moreover, they can unwittingly set limits on learning by unintentionally teaching children that they must be able to verbalize their thinking and have a rational plan for any activity that they undertake:

> *The demand that ideas always come with supporting arguments and explanations may lead one to reject out of hand thoughts that are in fact extremely fruitful, but which arrive without any indication of their pedigree or antecedents. The productive intuition can be overlooked in favour of the well-argued case.*

Thankfully, there is a growing awareness within education circles that children do indeed need to be allowed more time for processing and thinking, and that fostering 'thinking skills' is as important as imparting knowledge. There are many who believe that thinking skills need to be explicitly taught, and others who believe that they should be the underpinning of the curriculum, with as much attention paid to these skills as to content. It is through experimentation and subsequent mistakes that many of the world's greatest discoveries are made. Children need to be allowed the time and freedom to experiment and so learn from their successes and mistakes.

Planning time to 'hang out'
In addition to recognizing when individual children need to be allowed time to process and think, it is a good idea to actively plan for periods of time where everyone can simply 'hang out' and relax. For many people, this relaxation comes when they read a good book. For others, art is a relaxing, calming activity. Others like to listen to music or fiddle with beautiful artefacts such as beads, rocks, or stones. Toddlers often like to snuggle with an adult and a 'cuddly' of some sort, and many enjoy a gentle massage or having their hair stroked while doing something simple such as singing nursery rhymes. It is wise to resist the urge to keep children 'busy' all the time, and plan for regular relaxation times. Listening to a favourite story CD comfortably on cushions and bean bags can work for the whole group, or children can be offered a choice of painting, playing with small animals on the mat, or reading a book while calm music plays in the background. Giving this time a name such as 'Quiet Time' can help children to get the idea that this is a calm time where they can allow themselves to be still.

Thankfully, the EYFS is very clear that at all developmental stages, babies and children need time to rest, to think, and to pursue their own activities, unhurried by adults, while still feeling safe and secure:

> *Give time for children to pursue their learning without interruption, and to return to activities.*

Practice Guidance, DCSF, 2008

Those practitioners working with the youngest children need to consciously monitor the amount of stimulation that may be given, either intentionally or unintentionally. Sometimes the activity level surrounding the baby or toddler can become too much, whether or not she displays signs of discomfort. Telephones, televisions, background music, the busy-ness of everyday life, and the activity level of other children can sometimes overwhelm the senses of

a baby or toddler, and so it is a good idea to plan for regular quiet times for these youngest children. A snuggle time with a story or a soothing bath can help young children to develop the lifelong skills of calm and relaxation – with the added advantage of forcing the adult carers to take time to breathe and relax too!

A sad fact about life in the twenty-first century is that many children simply do not know how to relax. Maybe it is time for practitioners to see relaxation as a skill to be taught. Incorporating yoga into the daily routine is becoming a popular practice, with professional yoga centres now offering accredited training for early years providers. Yoga can be used to support all of the early learning goals. It can be undertaken as a calming relaxation activity on its own, or as a starting point for a game, a discussion, a story time, a music session or a maths activity. Whatever the context, a successful yoga programme will improve children's wellbeing:

> *Yoga is becoming increasingly popular with children, parents and early years providers because it not only supports the physical and emotional development of children but also enables them to focus their minds, develop improved concentration and to actively acquire the ability to relax their bodies. Over time children begin to value stillness and peacefulness by becoming better connected with themselves and the world around them.*

Farah-Naz Khan, co-founder, Yoga4UK Ltd.[113]

Other teachers use music during relaxation times, where they teach children how to slow their bodies and minds as they relax. Another antidote to the rush of many children's lives is to allow ample time for reading. In contrast to the media, which over-stimulates children, reading encourages the child to enter another imaginary world where she can relax physically and mentally. Reading should not be restricted to scheduled story or reading times. There should be many unscheduled spontaneous reading sessions throughout the week. Reading aloud with expression is becoming a lost art, and children need to hear a richness of language, content and ideas. David Elkind expresses the desirability of giving children time to read in his book *The Hurried Child*:

> *Regardless of the cycles in the focus of children's fiction, reading will remain a healthy counterpoise to hurrying and stress. Reading is under children's control and they can make their own choices and proceed at their own pace. Young people can and do find books that are nicely suited to where they are in their social and emotional development. In the larger world over which young people have so little control, the smaller world of books is a welcome oasis.*[114]

What a wonderful thing it would be to see children regularly basing their imaginary games upon characters from children's literature, rather than those from fast-moving TV shows or computer games. This will only happen if adults take an active role in introducing them to these literary characters and encouraging them to act out their favourite stories in their games.

To stem the tide of the stressful side effects of this new century, adults need to actively plan for children to relax – and to be kids! If they do this, the effect will be one of 'raising standards' both academically and socially. Children will stop feeling stressed through the pressure of doing too much, too soon. It takes courage to take a stand and allow children time to grow. If we have faith in the awesome capacity of the brain and we allow it to do its job without giving it time limits, we can raise standards simply by providing opportunities for children to think, process and learn in peace.

Plenary

Here are some points for reflection:

How flexible is your planning and your timetable, and how does it allow for you to be spontaneous and creative? How do you follow up on children's interests and extend their learning?

How well do the children in your setting cooperate in pairs or groups? How much opportunity do they get for group-work? How do you ensure that they learn the skills that are necessary for success in a group?

Can you identify which children in your setting are strongly visual, auditory or kinesthetic learners? What learning style do you personally prefer? How do you cater for the different types of learners in your setting and how do you help children to develop all three styles regardless of their preference?

Which of the multiple intelligences is your greatest strength? Do you value all eight intelligences equally? Is it clear to the children that you do so? Can you identify the multiple intelligence strengths of the children in your care? How do you cater for their individual learning needs? How do you ensure that there is a breadth and richness in the curriculum that you offer?

Do some of the children in your care seem overscheduled or stressed from the demands put upon them? If so, how do you compensate for this? Do the children in your setting get a chance to regularly interact with nature? Do you observe children before stepping in to discuss their learning with them? Do you plan for relaxation time? Do children in your setting need to be taught strategies for relaxation?

Where do we go from here?

Now that you have almost reached the end of this book, you have completed the first part of the brain-based journey. But the learning is only just beginning! When you put into practice the techniques that you have read about here, you will discover even more about the child's brain and learning.

Hopefully you now feel enthusiastic about beginning to put these ideas into practice in your setting. Do this at your own pace and in the order that makes most sense to you – there is no right or wrong way to introduce these techniques into any setting. After a time, you will look back and feel inspired by what you and the children in your care have learned and achieved.

Learning is a lifelong journey, full of excitement and adventure. May the journey be both rewarding and enjoyable, and may you and the children in your care have every success along the way!

Some useful websites

www.acceleratedlearning.co.uk – Nicola Call's website. This website gives more information about brain-based learning and updated information about books and resources. There is also a link for contacting Nicola directly

www.opitus.uk.com – Sally Featherstone's website where you can find information about her writing, courses and training. You can also email her directly at sally @opitus.uk.com

www.dcsf.gov.uk – For current government initiatives in education

www.publications.dcsf.gov.uk – For all government publications

www.qcda.gov.uk – For curriculum and assessment information in England

www.standards.dfes.gov.uk/thinkingskills – DCSF site for thinking in primary classrooms

www.teachers.tv – For TV, video and information on teaching at all ages and stages

www.early-education.org.uk – The website of the British Association for Early Childhood Education, a voluntary organization

www.inclusion.org.uk – The website for Inclusion UK – a consortium of four organizations supporting inclusion in education

www.thegraycenter.org – Website for The Gray Center, a non-profit organization dedicated to individuals with autism spectrum disorders, in particular through the development of Social Stories™

www.alite.co.uk – Alistair Smith's website. Useful site for brain-based articles and publications, researching training options, and purchasing resources. Alistair is one of the UK's leading trainers in brain-based learning

www.braingym.com – The official Brain Gym® website

www.brainresearch.com – An extensive website about brain research, with hundreds of links to related websites and articles

www.creative-partnerships.com – Creative Partnerships fosters innovative, long-term partnerships between schools and creative professionals, including artists, performers, architects, multimedia developers and scientists

www.foundation-stage.info – A site with articles, links and an early years discussion forum

www.richardlouv.com – The official website of Richard Louv, author of *Last Child in the Woods*, with a wealth of information about ways to protect childhood

www.suepalmer.co.uk – Sue Palmer's website, with information on publications and links to articles in various publications

www.naturalchild.org – The website for The Natural Child Project, whose motto is 'All children behave as well as they are treated.' Interesting articles about child development and the respectful care of young children

www.dana.org – The website for the Dana Foundation and the Dana Alliance, an organization of scientists dedicated to advancing education about brain research

www.jlcbrain.com – Eric Jensen's website containing information about training, publications and subscription to a monthly newsletter

www.circle-time.co.uk – The website for Jenny Mosley's 'Quality Circle Time', containing answers to frequently asked questions about circle time, some free resources and online bookshop

www.tactyc.org.uk – Training, Advancement and Co-operation in Teaching Young Children

Bibliography

Abbott, Lesley and Nutbrown, Cathy (eds), *Experiencing Reggio Emilia,* Open University Press, 2001

Ballinger, Erich, *The Learning Gym,* Edu-Kinesthetics, 1996

Basic Skills Agency, *Securing Boys' Literacy,* Basic Skills Agency, Tel 0870 600 2400

Biddulph, Steve, *Raising Babies – Why Your Love is Best*, HarperThorsons, 2006

Biddulph, Steve, *The Secret of Happy Children,* Thorsons; Harper Collins Publishers, 1998

Biddulph, Steve, *Raising Boys*, Thorsons, 2003

Bilton, Helen, *Outdoor Play in the Early Years*, David Fulton, 1998

Boyd Cadwell, Louise, *Bringing Reggio Emilia Home,* Teachers College Press, 1997

Brewer, Chris and Campbell, Don, *Rhythms of Learning,* Zephyr 1991

Bruce, Tina, *Learning through Play, Babies, Toddlers and the Foundation Years*, Hodder and Stoughton, 2001

Bunting, Madeline, *Willing Slaves – How The Overwork Culture Is Ruling Our Lives*, Harper Perennial, 2005

Buzan, Tony with Buzan, Barry, *The Mind Map Book – How to Use Radiant Thinking to Maximize Your Brain's Untapped Potential*, Penguin Books, 1993

Campbell, Don, *The Mozart Effect, Tapping the Power of Music to Heal the Body, Strengthen the Mind, and Unlock the Creative Spirit*, HarperCollins Publishers Inc, 1997

Campbell, Don, *The Mozart Effect for Children – Awakening Your Child's Mind, Health, and Creativity with Music*, HarperCollins Publishers, Inc, 2000

Ceppi and Zini, *Children, Spaces, Relationships – Metaproject for an Environment for Young Children*, Reggio Children, 1999

Claxton, Guy, Hare Brain, *Tortoise Mind – How Intelligence Increases When you Think Less*, HarperPerennial, 2000

Cousins, Jacqui, *Listening to Four Year Olds,* National Early Years Network, 1999

De Becker, Gavin, *Protecting the Gift – Keeping Children and Teenagers Safe (and Parents Sane)*, Dell Publishing, 1999

Dennison Paul E. and Gail E., *Brain Gym,* Edu-Kinesthetics, 1989

Donaldson, Margaret, *Children's Minds,* Penguin

Dweck, Carol S., Ph.D., *Mindset – The New Psychology of Success*, Random House, 2006

Eliot, Lise, Ph.D., *What's Going on in There? How the Brain and Mind Develop in the First Five Years* of life, Bantam Books, 2000

Elkind, David, Ph.D., The *Hurried Child – Growing Up Too Fast Too Soon*, Perseus Publishing, 2001

Gardner, Howard, *Frames of Mind – The Theory of Multiple Intelligences*, BasicBooks, 1993

Gardner, Howard, *Intelligence Reframed – Multiple Intelligences for the 21st Century*, Basic Books, 1999

Goer, Henci, *The Thinking Woman's Guide to a Better Birth,* The Berkley Publishing Group, 1999

Goldschmeid, Elinor, Elfer, Peter, and Selleck, Dorothy, *Key Persons in the Nursery: Building Relationships for Quality Provision*, David Fulton Publishers, 2003

Goleman, Daniel, *Emotional Intelligence, Why It Can Matter More Than IQ*, Bloomsbury Publishing Plc, 1995

Gopnik, Alison, Meltzoff, Andrew, and Patricia Kuhl, *How Babies Think,* The Orion Publishing Group Ltd, 1999

Gottman, John, *The Heart of Parenting,* Bloomsbury, 1997

Greenman, Jim, *Caring Spaces, Learning Places: Children's Environments That Work*, Exchange Press, 1988

Greenspan, Stanley M.D., *Building Healthy Minds – The Six Experiences that Create Intelligence and Emotional Growth in Babies and Young Children*, Perseus Publishing, 1999

Gurian, Michael, *Boys and Girls Learn Differently!*, Jossey Bass, 2002

Hannaford Carla, Ph.D., *Smart Moves – Why Learning is not all in your Head,* Great Ocean Publishers, 1995

Hart, Betty and Risley, Todd, *Meaningful Differences in the Everyday Experience of Young American Children*, Paul H Brookes Pub Co, 1995

Harter, Susan, 'Teacher and Classmate Influences on Scholastic Motivation, Self-esteem, and Level of Voice in Adolescents', in J. Juvonen and K. R. Wentzel (eds), *Social Motivation, Understanding Children's School Adjustment*, Cambridge University Press, 1996

Healy, Jane M., Ph.D., *Endangered Minds – Why Children Don't Think – and What We Can Do About It*, Touchstone Books, Simon & Schuster, 1990

Healy, Jane, Ph.D, *Failure to Connect – How Computers Affect our Children's Minds – for Better and Worse*, Simon and Schuster, 1998

Hendrick, Joanne, *The Whole Child,* Prentice-Hall Inc, 1996

Howe, Christine, *Gender and Classroom Interaction – A Research Review,* The Scottish Council for Research in Education, 1997

Jensen, Eric, *Teaching with the Brain in Mind*, ASDC (USA), 1998

Jossey Bass Reader on the Brain and Learning, Jossey-Bass Publishers, 2008

Kohn, Alfie, *Punished by Rewards – The Trouble with Gold Stars, Incentive Plans, As, Praise and Other Bribes*, Houghton Mifflin Company, New York, 1993

Kohn, Alfie, *Unconditional Parenting – Moving from Rewards and Punishments to Love and Reason*, Atria Books, 2005

Kotulak, Ronald, *Inside the Brain. Revolutionary Discoveries of How the Mind Works*, Andrews McMeel Publishing, 1997

Lindstrom, Martin, *Brand child – Remarkable Insights into the Minds of Today's Global Kids and Their Relationships with Brands*, Kogan Page Limited, 2003

Louv, Richard, *Last Child in the Woods – Saving Our Children from Nature-Deficit Disorder*, Algonquin Books of Chapel Hill, 2006

Miles, Elizabeth, *Tune Your Brain – Using Music to Manage Your Mind, Body and Mood*, Berkley Publishing Group, 1997

Miller, Judy, *Never Too Young – How Young Children can take Responsibility and make Decisions*, National Early Years Network, 1996

Mosley, Jenny, *Quality Circle Time in the Primary Classroom*, LDA, 1999

Nutbrown, Cathy, *Threads of Thinking*, Paul Chapman, 1999

Ouvry, Marjorie, *Exercising Muscles and Minds*, National Early Years Network, 2000

Palmer, Sue, *Toxic Childhood – How the Modern World is Damaging our Children and What We Can Do About It*, Orion Books Ltd, 2007

Pantley, Elizabeth, *Hidden Messages – What Our Words and Actions are Really Telling Our Children*, Contemporary Books, 2001

Pascal Chris and Bertram Tony, *Effective Early Learning* (Case Studies in Improvement), Hodder & Stoughton, 1997

Paul, Pamela, *Parenting Inc. – How We Are Sold on $800 Strollers, Fetal Education, Baby Sign Language, Sleeping Coaches, Toddler Couture, and Diaper Wipe Warmers – and What it Means for Our Children*, Times Books, 2008

Reggio Children, *The Hundred Languages of Children*, Reggio Children, 1996

Richardson, Gail Ryder, *Creating a Space to Grow – Developing Your Outdoor Learning Environment*, David Fulton Publishers Ltd, 2006

Roehlkepartain and Leffert, *What Children need to Succeed*, Free Spirit, EY Network, 1996

Schiller, Pam, *Start Smart! Building Brain Power in the Early Years*, Gryphon House, Inc, 1999

Sears, William, MD and Sears, Martha, RN, *The Baby Book*, Little, Brown and Company, 1993

Smith, Alistair, *The Brain's Behind It – New Knowledge About the Brain and Learning*, Network Educational Press Ltd, 2002

Tizard, Barbara and Hughes, Martin, *Young Children Learning*, Harvard University Press, 1984

Trythall, Andrew, *Managing ICT from Birth to 7*, Featherstone Education Ltd, 2006

The Thinking Child — Brain-based learning for the foundation stage

References

1. Kotulak, Ronald, *Inside the Brain: Revolutionary Discoveries of How the Mind Works*. Andrews McMeel Publishing, Kansas City, 1997

2. Schnur, Tatiana 'Area Of Brain Key To Choosing Words Identified', *Science Daily*, December 2008, at http://www.sciencedaily.com

3. Goodwin, Frederick, quoted by Kotulak, Ronald, *Inside the Brain: Revolutionary Discoveries of How the Mind Works*. Andrews McMeel Publishing, 1997

4. Montessori, Maria, *The Absorbent Mind*. Henry Holt, 1995

5. Richards, M., et al. 'Birth weight and cognitive function in the British 1946 birth cohort: longitudinal population based study'. *British Medical Journal*, 27 Jan 2001

6. Darwin, Charles, 'Chapter 2 – On the Manner of Development of Man from Some Lower Form', *The Descent of Man*. Prometheus Books (reprint edition), 1997

7. Research quoted by Kotulak, Ronald. Paper presented in Chicago to the conference 'Brain Development in Young Children: New Frontiers for Research, Policy and Practice', 13 June 1996

8. Biddulph, Steve, *The Secret of Happy Children*. Thorsons; HarperCollins Publishers, 1998

9. Crawford, C., Dearden, L. and Meghir, C., *When You Are Born Matters: The Impact of Date of Birth on Child Cognitive Outcomes in England*. Institute for Fiscal Studies, 2007

10. Work of Gage, Fred H. (Salk Institute, California) and Eriksson, Peter S. (Göteborg University, Sweden), *The Scientific American*, November 1998

11. Anderson, James W., *The American Journal of Clinical Nutrition*, October 1999

12. Dennison Paul E. and Gail E., Brain Gym, Edu-Kinesthetics Inc, 1989

13. Penn State Children's Hospital, Reuters, quoted at www.cosmiverse.com

14. *National Languages Strategy*, DfES, 2002

15. Research by Sapolsky, Robert, quoted in Kotulak, Ronald, *Inside the Brain: Revolutionary Discoveries of How the Mind Works*. Andrews McMeel Publishing, 1997

16. *Statutory Framework for the Early Years Foundation Stage, Welfare Requirements*, DCSF, May 2008

17. Department of Health, *Our Healthier Nation: A Contract for Health*. Green Paper, 1998

18. Pollitt, E. 'Annual Review of Nutrition', *Iron Deficiency and Cognitive Function*. Vol. 13: 521–537, 1993

19. James, J. A. and Laing, G. J., 'Iron Deficiency Anemia', *Current Pediatrics*, 1994

20. McNay, Ewan C., Fries, Thomas M. and Gold, Paul E., 'Decreases in rat extracellular hippocampal glucose concentration associated with cognitive demand during a spatial task', *Proceedings of the National Academy of Sciences of the United States of America*, Vol. 97, No. 6, 14 March 2000

21. Research by Andrew Scholey et al. (University of Northumbria and the Cognitive Research Unit), Reading, presented to a symposium at the British Psychological Society's annual conference in Blackpool, 13 March 2002, www.uk.news.yahoo.com

22. Lavigne, John V. et al., *Journal of Developmental and Behavioral Pediatrics*, June 2000

23. Coe, C. L., Glass, J. C., Wiener, S. G. and Levine, S., 'Behavioral, but not Physiological: Adaptation to Repeated Separation in Mother and Infant Primates', *Psychoneuroendocrinology*, 8(4): 401–409, 1983. Cited in API News, Vol. 5, No. 1, 2002

24. *Health Survey for England 2005 Latest Trends, Key Facts*, NHS, 20 December 2006

25. *Healthy Weight, Healthy Lives: Six Months On*, Department of Children, Schools and Families and Department of Health, 2008

26. Gillespie, Kathleen, M., Gale, Edwin A. M. and Bingley, Polly J. (Division of Medicine,

University of Bristol, Bristol), 'High Familial Risk and Genetic Susceptibility in Early Onset Childhood Diabetes Department of Diabetes and Metabolism', *Diabetes*, Vol. 51, January 2002

27. Wolf, David Bernard and Parker, Philip A., 'If all the Raindrops', SBK Records, 1993

28. University of Minnesota, 'Regular Family Meals Promote Healthy Eating Habits', in *Science Daily*, November 2004

29. *A School Report Card: Consultation Document*, DCSF and Ofsted, 2008

30. Centre for Studies on Inclusive Education, www.inclusion.org.uk

31. *Improving the Life Chances of Disabled People*, Prime Minister's Strategy Unit, January 2005

32. The National Autistic Society at www.nas.org.uk

33. Galloway, John, *Ask the Experts, The Accessible Curriculum*, http://inclusion.ngfl.gov.uk, December 2008

34. The Foundation Stage Forum at www.foundation-stage.info

35. In the Picture, www.childreninthepicture.org.uk

36. Goleman, Daniel, *Emotional Intelligence, Why It Can Matter More Than IQ*, Bloomsbury Publishing Plc, 1995

37. *Excellence and Enjoyment: Social and Emotional Aspects of Learning*, DfES, 2005

38. Kohn, Alfie, *Unconditional Parenting – Moving from Rewards and Punishments to Love and Reason*, Atria Books, 2005

39. Schellenberg, Glenn E., 'Music Lessons Enhance IQ', *Psychological Science*, Vol. 15 I, No. 8, August 2004

40. Dweck, Carol S., Ph.D., *Mindset – The New Psychology of Success*, Random House, 2006

41. Mosley, Jenny, *Quality Circle Time in the Primary Classroom*, LDA, 1999

42. *Excellence and Enjoyment: Social and Emotional Aspects of Learning*, DfES, 2005

43. Hannaford, Carla, *Smart Moves, Why Learning is Not All in Your Head*, Great Ocean Publishers, 1995

44. Howe, Christine, *Gender and Classroom Interaction – A Research Review*, The Scottish Council for Research in Education, 1997

45. Kohn, Alfie, *Punished by Rewards – The Trouble with Gold Stars, Incentive Plans, As,* *Praise and Other Bribes*, Houghton Mifflin Company, New York, 1993

46. Details of the Bookstart programme can be found at www.surestart.gov.uk

47. Ghazvini, A. S. and Readdick, C. A., 1994, 'Parent-Caregiver Communication and Quality of Care in Diverse Child Care Settings', quoted in Joanne Hendrick, *The Whole Child*, Prentice-Hall Inc., 1996

48. 'Extended Schools: A Guide for Governors 1', COGS, NGA, NRT, ContinYou, 2006

49. Ibid.

50. Bowlby, John, *Maternal Care and Mental Health*, World Health Organization, 1951

51. Goldschmeid, Elinor, Elfer, Peter and Selleck, Dorothy, *Key Persons in the Nursery: Building Relationships for Quality Provision*, David Fulton, 2003

52. *The Effective Provision of Pre-School Education (EPPE) Project*, DfES, November 2004

53. Research carried out for the Equalities Review, reported in *The Guardian*, 15 July 2008

54. *Next Steps for Early Learning and Childcare; Building on the 10-year Strategy*, DCSF, 2009

55. Biddulph, Steve, *Raising Babies – Why Your Love is Best*, HarperThorsons, 2006

56. Bunting, Madeleine, 'Nursery Tales', *The Guardian*, 8 July 2004

57. Clarke, John Henrik, 'A Search for Identity', *Social Casework,* Vol. 51, No. 5: 259–264, May 1970

58. Kotulak, Ronald, *Inside the Brain – Revolutionary Discoveries of How the Mind Works*, Andrew McMeel, 1997

59. Castellanos, F. Xavier, MD et al., research presented in *Archives of General Psychiatry*, July 1996

60. Figures obtained under the Freedom of Information Act, quoted in Channel 4 News online, 17 July 2008

61. Figures obtained under the Freedom of Information Act, quoted in The Times Online, 18 June 2007

62. *The Observer*, 9 September 2001, quoted at www.guardian.co.uk

63. National Deaf Children's Society statistics; www.ndcs.org.uk

64. Kohn, Alfie, *Punished by Rewards – The Trouble with Gold Stars, Incentive Plans, As, Praise and Other Bribes*, Houghton Mifflin Company, New York, 1993

65. Gurian, Michael, *Boys and Girls Learn Differently!*, Jossey Bass, 2002

66. *The Final Report of the Independent Review of Mathematics Teaching in Early Years Settings and Primary Schools*, DCSF, June 2008

67. *Statutory Framework for the Early Years Foundation Stage*, DCSF, May 2008

68. *The Cambridge Education Review Final Report, Children, their World, their Education*, October 2009

69. Hart, Betty and Risley, Todd, *Meaningful Differences in the Everyday Experience of Young American Children*, Paul H Brookes, 1995

70. Quotation from University of Kansus; Office of University Relations website at www.ur.ku.edu

71. *Can do Better – Raising boys' Achievement in English*, Qualifications and Curriculum Authority, 1998

72. Buzan, Tony with Buzan, Barry *The Mind Map Book – How to Use Radiant Thinking to Maximize Your Brain's Untapped Potential*, Penguin Books, 1993

73. Berg, C. L. van den, Hol, T., Everts, H., Koolhaas, J. M., van Ree, J. M., Spruijt, B. M. (1999) 'Play is indispensable for an adequate development of coping with social challenges in the rat', *Developmental Psychobiology*, Vol. 34, 129–138

74. Greenspan, Stanley, M.D., *Building Healthy Minds – The Six Experiences that Create Intelligence and Emotional Growth in Babies and Young Children*, Perseus Publishing, 1999

75. Cousins, Jacqui, *Listening to Four Year Olds*, National Early Years Network, 1999

76. Lindstrom, Martin with Seybold, Patricia B., *BrandChild: Remarkable Insights into the Minds of Today's Global Kids and Their Relationships with Brands*, Kogan Page Ltd, 2005

77. Ryder Richardson, Gail, *Creating a Space to Grow – Developing Your Outdoor Learning Environment*, David Fulton Publishers Ltd, 2006

78. Campbell, Don, *The Mozart Effect for Children – Awakening Your Child's Mind, Health, and Creativity with Music*, HarperCollins Publishers, Inc., 2000

79. Wolff, I., Hurwitz, P. H., Bortnick, B. D., and Kokas, K. (1975) 'Nonmusical effects of the Kodaly music curriculum in primary grade children', *Journal of Learning Disabilities*, *MuSICA Research Notes*, Vol. 1, Issue 2.8, 45–51. www.musica.uci.edu

80. *Education Week*, 12 March 1997, www.edweek.org

81. Campbell, Don, *The Mozart Effect, Tapping the Power of Music to Heal the Body, Strengthen the Mind, and Unlock the Creative Spirit*, HarperCollins Publishers Inc., 1997

82. Research quoted in Campbell, Don, *The Mozart Effect, Tapping the Power of Music to Heal the Body, Strengthen the Mind, and Unlock the Creative Spirit*, HarperCollins Publishers Inc., 1997

83. Hannaford, Carla, Ph.D., *Smart Moves – Why Learning is Not All in Your Head*, Great Ocean Publishers, 1995

84. *Letters and Sounds, Primary National Strategy*, DfES, 2007

85. Jolly Learning at www.jollylearning.co.uk

86. Hannaford, Carla, Ph.D., *Smart Moves – Why Learning is Not All in Your Head*, Great Ocean Publishers, 1995

87. Trythall, Andrew, *Managing ICT from Birth to 7*, Featherstone Education Ltd, 2006

88. 'Talking Tins' can be found at http://www.talkingproducts.co.uk

89. Healy, Jane, Ph.D., *Failure to Connect – How Computers Affect our Children's Minds – for Better and Worse*, Simon and Schuster, 1998

90. Palmer, Sue, *Toxic Childhood – How the Modern World is Damaging our Children and What We Can Do About It*, Orion Books Ltd, 2007

91. Siraj-Blatchford, Iram, Sylva, Kathy, Muttock, Stella, Gilden, Rose and Bell, Danny, *Researching Effective Pedagogy in the Early Years*, DfES, 2002

92. Elkind, David, Ph.D., *The Hurried Child – Growing Up Too Fast Too Soon*, Perseus Publishing, 2001, Preface to Third Edition

93. Research quoted in Howe, Christine, *Gender and Classroom Interaction: A Research Review*. The Scottish Council for Research in Education, 1997

94. Rosenow, Nancy, 'Learning to love the Earth . . . and each other', *Journal of the National Association for the Education of Young Children*, Vol. 63 I, No.1, January 2008

95. Kutolak, Ronald, *Inside the Brain – Revolutionary Discoveries of how the Mind Works*, Andrew McMeel Publishing, 1997

96. Einstein, Albert, 1879–1955, German-born American physicist, author and Nobel Laureate

97. Holmes, Oliver Wendell, 1809–1894, American physician, professor and author

98. Eliot, Lise, Ph.D., *What's Going On In There? How the Brain and Mind Develop in the First Five Years of Life*, Bantam Books, 1999

99. Ibid.

100. Voltaire, François Marie Arouet de, 1694–1778, French author and philosopher

101. Gardner, Howard, *Intelligence Reframed – Multiple Intelligences for the 21st Century*, Basic Books, 1999

102. Claxton, Guy, *Hare Brain, Tortoise Mind, How Intelligence Increases When you Think Less*, HarperPerennial, 2000

103. Palmer, Sue, *Toxic Childhood – How the Modern World is Damaging our Children and What We Can Do About It*, Orion Books Ltd, 2007

104. Department for Education and Skills; Office for National Statistics, http://www.statistics.gov.uk/cci/nugget.asp?id=1766

105. Provision for Children under Five Years of Age in England: January 2007, DfES, May 2007, http://www.dfes.gov.uk/rsgateway/DB/SFR/s000729/SFR19–2007.pdf

106. Paul, Pamela, *Parenting Inc. – How We Are Sold on 4800 Strollers, Fetal Education, Baby Sign Language, Sleeping Coaches, Toddler Couture, and Diaper Wipe Warmers – and What It Means for Our Children*, Times Books, 2008

107. Palmer, Sue, *Toxic Childhood – How the Modern World is Damaging our Children and What We Can Do About It*, Orion Books Ltd, 2007

108. Elkind, David, Ph.D., *The Hurried Child – Growing Up Too Fast Too Soon*, Perseus Publishing, 2001

109. Gavin, De Becker, *Protecting the Gift, Keeping Children and Teenagers Safe (and Parents Sane)*, Dell Publishing, 1999

110. Louv, Richard, *Last Child in the Woods – Saving Our Children from Nature-Deficit Disorder*, Algonquin Books of Chapel Hill, 2006

111. *Independent Review of the Primary Curriculum: Final Report*, DCSF, 2009

112. Claxton, Guy, *Hare Brain, Tortoise Mind, How Intelligence Increases When you Think Less*, HarperPerennial, 2000

113. Khan, Farah-Naz, 'Calming Foundations', *Early Years Magazine*, October 2008

114. Elkind, David, Ph.D., *The Hurried Child – Growing Up Too Fast Too Soon*, Perseus Publishing, 2001, Preface to Third Edition

Index

The Thinking Child

Brain-based learning for the early years foundation stage